Collecting
Black
Americana

Collecting Black Americana

DAWN E. RENO

Photographs by Donald Vogt

Crown Publishers Inc., New York

With lots of love and appreciation for their support and understanding, this book is dedicated to my husband, Bobby, my daughter, Jennifer, and my friend and photographer's mate, Kristin

Published by Crown Publishers, Inc., 225 Park Avenue South, New York, New York 10003 and represented in Canada by the Canadian MANDA Group

CROWN is a trademark of Crown Publishers, Inc.

Manufactured in the United States of America

Library of Congress Cataloging-in-Publication Data

Reno, Dawn E.,
    Collecting Black Americana.

    Bibliography: p.
    Includes index.
    1. Afro-Americans—Collectibles.   I. Title.
II. Title: Black Americana.
NK839.3.A35R46   1986   700'.8996073'075   85-29968

ISBN 0-517-56095-X

10 9 8 7 6 5 4 3 2 1

First Edition

Contents

Introduction

When I first began noticing black collectibles, it was not necessarily because of their beauty or workmanship but rather because, as an antiques dealer, I saw the value they were commanding in a market just opening its eyes to the character and naiveté of country items and their "cousins."

Black doorstops, banks, dolls, and advertising items seemed to blend in well with the painted pine cupboards, trestle tables, and rough-hewn furniture that magazines everywhere were touting as the "country look." Even designers such as Ralph Lauren were beginning to add quilts, baskets, and homespun items to their displays. Country was chic! Items that had been around since before the Civil War but had been unnoticed until now were being assembled into collections worthy of the finer auction houses.

Folk art was riding a wave in the antiques world, commanding prices unheard of twenty years before. Art by and of the black people was being unearthed. After years of being relegated to the back of the closet, black items were finally commanding prices worthy of attention.

Although many collectors will tell you they have been accumulating black items for years, they will all admit to having no reference book available that categorized their finds. Many books on antiques may have had chapters that highlighted certain pieces of black folk art, banks, or kitchen collectibles with the familiar "Mammy" figure, but nowhere was there a book encompassing all the different avenues a collector of black Americana could pursue.

Some will argue that most of the items falling into these categories are racist or degrading to black people. They are right. Unfortunately, this is part of our heritage and part of the history of the American black. It is also one of the reasons why certain pieces of black Americana are worth so much more than others.

Whatever the reasons one finds to collect items of a black nature, we can all be sure that black collectibles are pieces of our history that need to be recorded, because we will not see the likes of them again.

The information compiled in this volume only scratches the surface of what is available in the United States. We have not even begun to discover what there is in the rest of the world.

The work is not yet done. There is much to be discovered and more treasures to be documented. But we have made the first efforts and will continue to learn more with each passing day, from each collector or dealer we meet.

To all of those who have contributed information, photographs, or just plain support, I thank you heartily. To those of you who welcomed Donald and me into your homes and shops, we will never forget you and the discoveries we made together. We have learned a lot from you, the dealer, the collector, the museums and colleges, and the interested bystander. We know there is much, much more to be learned. We hope you will be there to learn with us.

Advertising giveaway, lithographed cardboard nursery toy, late nineteenth century. *Collection of/photo by Evelyn Ackerman.*

1

Advertising

Advertising, a form of communication intended to promote the sale of a product or service, was first begun in ancient times when a public crier roamed the streets calling attention to the sale of slaves, cattle, or imports. Yet when we talk about collecting advertising that depicts blacks, what we are, in effect, discussing is prejudice.

Early advertising was the strongest medium through which American white businessmen could express their feelings toward American blacks and seek to keep control over those people they considered their slaves.

Overgeneralized statements were brought to the public's eye via pictures used to advertise commonly used products. These pictures, colorfully produced on boxes, cans, bottles, trade cards, and posters, depicted the black person as a cotton worker, butler, maid, cook, waitress, laundress, or just plain "ol' poo' people." Nowhere in early advertising does one find a black family depicted as a hard-working, loving group.

Not until businessmen realized there was a black market, a black consumer, did they change their advertising principles. Thus, misconceptions lodged in the public's collective brain by crafty advertising dynamos remained there unchanged for hundreds of years.

The child growing up in the home of an average Northern family may not have been *taught* to hate the black race, but more than likely the child *caught* the basic principle of prejudice through day-to-day living. Mother used Fun-to-Wash soap to do the laundry (wasn't the old black woman whose face covered the front of the box funny-looking?). Mother often served coffee bought in cans decorated with black figures in their native costumes. When she bought material to make the family clothes, her thread would come with a trade card that her little daughter could have to paste in her album. ("Do all little nigger children have torn clothes, Mommy?")

When the ads became more explicit and their "characters" talked, it was always in a bastardized version of the English language. Such is the way prejudice is taught and maintained as a standard way of life.

Prejudice in advertising was the norm before the Civil War ended and blacks were free to begin their own communities, build their own homes and businesses, and become consumers. Yet advertisers were slow to pick up on the change in the black person's buying power.

During the nineteenth century, advertising prospered. The Industrial Revolution had a great impact on the advertising trade. The output of factories was greater and advertising helped to sell the extra products. Magazines and newspapers were sold worldwide, bringing about innovation after innovation in the way salable items were marketed. Black-owned newspapers, too, began buying advertising, and though their markets were smaller and the dollars budgeted for advertising not the big amounts the national magazines and newspapers commanded, still the move toward pleasing the black consumer had begun.

This is not to say that advertising that degraded blacks had completely stopped. Far from it! Bottles, cans, posters, and boxes still showed the black person in undignified poses and advertisers continued to profit from their use of these symbols to advertise their products. However, the choices were more subtle than before. The characters' features were a little less pronounced; the language quoted was a little closer to what the Northern white used on a daily basis. Instead of being treated as hated slaves, strangers from a foreign land, blacks were now being depicted as children, pets, or ignorant people who were to be pitied.

In some early advertising manuals, advertisers were advised to keep in mind that they were dealing with the Negro group and to remember that the Negro was a "simple-souled individual, little interested in or appreciating other appeals than price."

During the 1920s and 1930s, tests were made to see how advertising appealed to black consumers. Companies would run two ads, both with different illustrations, to test the response. One ad would show white women (or men) using or discussing a certain product. The other ad would feature a black person discussing the same product. Each individual was tested to see which ad got and held his/her attention.

Naturally, the ads featuring black people gained the attention of most people—in fact, almost 80 percent of the respondents showed their approval. As a result, the advertising world began to shift emphasis from all-white advertising and degrading use of Negroes in advertising to the use of the everyday black person in their ads. The trend is still moving toward incorporating blacks into each ad campaign that a major company launches.

Advertising poster for Mil-Kay Vitamin Drinks, approximately 12″ × 8″. *Courtesy of Rose Fontanella; photo by Donald Vogt.*

Until the 1940s and 1950s, advertising aimed at the Negro's buying power was given little or no thought. Stores seeking to attract black customers used local dailies to hawk their goods instead of putting their advertising dollars into glossy magazines, which the "modern colored person" might never read or be able to afford. Negro weekly newspapers received most of the copy designed to entice the black buying public.

Once companies realized the sales value of racial elements in their advertising copy, more firms employed a central black figure in their advertising. Aunt Jemima became almost a historical figure; a subordinate cleaning woman was used in Rinso detergent ads; and the Gold Dust twins, a pair of nearly naked black children, graced the front of that detergent box.

Dissension with the way Negroes were used in advertising began in the 1930s and grew stronger with the passing of years. Prominent black people began expressing their displeasure with the way blacks were used in advertising. Among their complaints were the facts that blacks were being used to advertise white men's products, thus making the white man rich;

that the blacks used in ads were not made up well and did not show the Negro in complimentary ways; and that for some Americans, these ads, radio shows, and plays constituted their first impression of the black race.

Thus, it is true that when we speak of the black American in advertising, we speak of prejudice.

TYPES OF COLLECTIBLE ADVERTISING

ADS

Ads depicting blacks can be found in the earliest American newspapers and are fairly common throughout the published pieces one may pick up at an antiques show, shop, or garage sale.

Usually the rare ads are also the ones that are the most degrading to the black race. Although one might think that this type of ad can be found only in periodicals dating before the Civil War, ads from the 1920s to 1940s are often so slanderous to the black people that if they were to be found today, a lawsuit would be the next step.

Often you can tell by the style of an ad when it was published. Knowing the differences between pre–Civil War, Civil War, Victorian, Art Nouveau, and Art Deco styles will help you to date your ad. A few other points to remember are that women were popular in ads at the time of the Civil War, company buildings were popular around 1880, and advertising using blacks began before the Civil War and continued through the 1940s. The style of dress can also give you a clue to age, as will the mode of transportation used in the ad. Should you be lucky enough to find the complete periodical where your ad was published, you will find the date on the front page.

BOTTLES AND BOXES

Nicolas Appert, a Parisian confectioner, was the first to succeed using glass bottles to preserve foods in 1810. However, paper labels were not used until much later. The most common collectible bottles depicting blacks were not made until the turn of the century, with the bulk of them produced in the 1920s and later. Utica Club Ale bottles show a young black waiter; other bottles, especially liquor bottles, may show blacks in similar lowly positions.

The earliest advertising boxes were metal pieces that were painted or stenciled. It was not until 1850 that the Somers Brothers of Brooklyn, New York, invented a method of lithographing a design onto a metal box. Lithographed pieces are very popular and worth more if they have pictures on them.

Cardboard boxes to hold soap powder or spices began to be produced after the Industrial Revolution and were often printed by the hundreds. There are still times when a dealer or collector may come up with an unused carton of Fun-to-Wash boxes, although the collector should beware as these advertising pieces are now being reproduced and the copies are hard to distinguish from the originals.

TINS

Tins with paper labels are difficult to find in good condition. Occasionally, as with boxes, a dealer or collector will come upon a box of unused labels. Do question their validity, but take into consideration the fact that these pieces were manufactured in bulk and often left in storage when a company went out of business or changed its style of advertising.

Rarity and condition determine the price of most tins, but shape is also a factor. For example, a three-dimensional shape is more highly valued than the traditional round, while the roly-poly is the most desirable of all.

The roly-poly tins were made to resemble people. One was a rotund black woman called "Mammy." They were made in 1912–1913 and there are at least two versions of the Mammy roly-poly.

Listerine ad, January 1941. *Courtesy of Gwendolyn Goldman; photo by Donald Vogt.*

Coffee cans often had black figures in their advertising. It appeared to be the vogue to advertise coffee by showing blacks from the islands with turbans wrapped around their heads and brightly colored clothes on their bodies. Of particular note when dating coffee cans: the words "Java" and "Mocha" could be used before 1906, but after 1906—the year the Pure Food and Drug Act was passed—all claims had to be true, so the words disappeared. Although Luzianne Coffee is probably the most familiar of these cans, one could spend the rest of one's collecting life just trying to find all the figures that were used to advertise coffee.

When collecting tins, it is important to remember—as with all antiques—that condition is paramount. Therefore, cleaning should be well thought out and attempted only when *absolutely necessary*.

TRADE CARDS

Colorful advertising cards, commonly known as trade cards, were given to the purchaser of articles such as shoes, thread, and household items just before and especially during the Victorian era. The cards were saved and sometimes pasted into an album that every member of the family could enjoy.

Advertising tins for International Harness Soap and Carter's Inky Racer, both made during the late 1800s, feature Black figures. *Courtesy of Rose Fontanella; photo by Donald Vogt.*

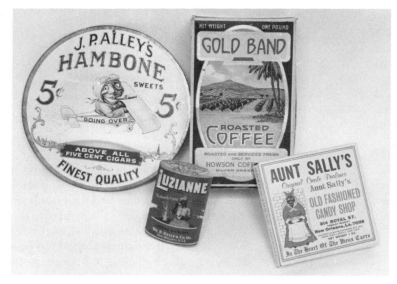

From left to right: Hambone 5¢ cigar label, Luzianne Coffee coupon, Gold Band Roasted Coffee label, Aunt Sally's candy box. *Courtesy of Jeanie Ohle; photo by Donald Vogt.*

(Right)
Advertising tin for Mammy's Favorite Brand Coffee, C. D. Kenny Co., Baltimore, Md., 4-lb. size. *Photo by Donald Vogt.*

Condition of trade cards is all-important. Rips, stains, holes, or dog-eared corners are considerations one must understand when purchasing a card. If any one of these defects appears on the card you are about to purchase, keep in mind that any damage lowers the value of paper goods.

Trade cards depicting blacks started to show up in the early 1800s as lithographers in Boston, New York, Philadelphia, and Baltimore began printing trade cards to advertise every product imaginable. Some of the cards were fairly acceptable, but others were racist and extremely derogatory. One unusually degrading trade card depicts Frederick Douglass with his second wife, a white woman, taking Sulpher Bitters to lighten his skin.

Negro trade card sales have risen dramatically in the last ten years, causing their values to skyrocket. A card that was worth $2 in 1978 could easily triple in value over as short a period as four years—an incredible price jump, even in the antiques world.

Although some of the sayings on trade cards depicting blacks are insulting, that fact seems to have increased, rather than decreased, their value. The cards show Negroes in compromising or lowly positions, as large-headed, pop-eyed models helping to advertise items such as cotton seeds, coffee, and complexion creams.

The Fairbanks Company made a card showing a white child asking a poorly dressed black child, "Why doesn't your Mama wash you with Fairy Soap?"

Rising Sun Stove Polish made a series of comical trade cards depicting the devastating effects on households that did not use their stove polish. One such card shows a black woman exclaiming, "Look yere old man! What kind o' stove blacking you call dat? I'se been rubbin' on dat stove all mornin' an' it don't gib it a polish worf a cent. You jest git de Rising Sun Stove Polish right away or dar'l be trouble. You think I got time to 'speriment with such mud?"

The bottom half of the card shows the woman happily welcoming her man: "Come in, Ephraim! I'se not mad with you dis time, case yer sent me de genuine Rising Sun Stove Blacking; an it shines de stove in good shape. An' here's yer dinner all ready. Somethin' agin ye? No, deed I haven't; yer tink I'se an anjul to get along without good stove polish?"

FIRMS THAT USED BLACKS IN THEIR ADVERTISING

The Aunt Jemima Pancake Flour Company used quite a few different objects in their promotions, all of which depicted the jolly black woman in her red turban. Salt and pepper shakers, cookie jars, plastic and cardboard items, even a pottery set of kitchen condiment holders made by the Weller Pottery company, were given away in their promotions.

The Bull Durham Tobacco Company used blacks in most of their advertising. One can find groups of black men engaged in card games, throwing dice, or just rocking on the porch, in

Child-size red pancake grill with white-and-brown advertising (model R-601), used by Quaker Oats to advertise Aunt Jemima Pancake Mix. *Courtesy of Judy Posner; photo by Donald Vogt.*

Bull Durham's advertising posters. These posters have been reproduced and have been seen selling for $500 and up. Buyer beware!

Who can forget the *Cream of Wheat* chef? His smiling face has adorned the cereal's ads and boxes from the early 1900s to this day. Earlier in this century, one could find ads for Cream of Wheat in every magazine and newspaper. "Rastus" was so popular that the company even had dolls made in his likeness as promotional giveaways. Most Cream of Wheat ads are very pleasing and can be framed and hung on a picture wall.

Coon Chicken Inn Restaurants were a chain of eating places throughout Seattle, Washington, Portland, Oregon, and Salt Lake City, Utah. The restaurants were in existence from 1924 through the early 1950s and were recognizable by the large, smiling porter's face that adorned the front of each. Patrons entered the establishment through the porter's mouth. Menus, plates, napkins, and so forth from the chain are considered highly collectible.

Fun-to-Wash soap powder boxes depict a "Mammy" face on the front of the box. She wears a large grin and a scarf wrapped around her head. There are still factory cases of unused boxes, some with soap in them, still on the market.

Gold Dust Washing Powder showed a pair of black children running across the front of the box. A number of other objects, from figures to toys, were made in the Gold Dust twins' image. The detergent boxes are orange with black lettering and come in several sizes.

"Getting Up Steam," ad for Cream of Wheat. *Courtesy of Gwendolyn Goldman; photo by Donald Vogt.*

Toothpick holders from the Coon Chicken Inn. The one on the right has been repainted. *Courtesy of Jan Thalberg; photo by Donald Vogt.*

Gold Dust Twins Washing Powder ad, May 1906. *Courtesy of Gwendolyn Goldman; photo by Donald Vogt.*

Green River Whiskey used an old black man astride a mule in its advertising campaigns. The company made store display pieces as well as liquor decanters and used them extensively.

Luzianne Coffee's lady is perhaps one of the best-known black advertising symbols. The figure, clad in a green skirt and short-sleeved top, a scarf around her head, has withstood time and remained the symbol everyone associates with Luzianne. Figurines, spice sets, sample giveaways, and tins can be found featuring her image. One must remember that the Luzianne lady with the green skirt is the original. There are reproductions on the market with a different colored skirt.

Pickanninny Brand Peanut Butter was decorated with a black girl on the front of the can. The small pail of peanut butter was in use in the 1920s. Prices for the pail can go as high as several hundred dollars.

Utica Club Soda used a black waiter holding a tray with a bottle of Utica Club perched on it. He was usually shown on the front label used in their bottling.

Advertising piece for Green River Whiskey, wood, 1910–1920. *Courtesy of Malinda Saunders; photo by Donald Vogt.*

A hard-to-find sample-size Luzianne Coffee tin in good shape. *Courtesy of Jeanie Ohle; photo by Donald Vogt.*

Three Utica Club beverage bottles show how a black waiter was used in their advertising for many years. *Courtesy of Rose Fontanella; photo by Donald Vogt.*

ITEM DESCRIPTION   APPROXIMATE PRICE

Ad, Cream of Wheat, "Getting Up Steam," June 1924 .... $10–$15

Ad, Cream of Wheat, nursery rhyme series, Old King Cole .... $18–$22

Ad, Cream of Wheat, "Oh, I done forgot dat Cream of Wheat" .... $45–$55

Ad, Cream of Wheat, "What do you charge for board, sir?" .... $10–$15

Ad, Gold Dust Twins, May 1906 .... $5–$7

Ad, Harper's Weekly, framed, New Orleans Centennial Exposition, December 1884 .... $65–$75

Ad, Listerine, black family, January 1941 .... $5–$7

Ad, Paramount Kid, April 1906 .... $5–$7

Ad, Picanninny Freeze, cardboard, girl with watermelon, "Picanninny Freeze 5¢" .... $30–$40

Ad, Post Toasties, August 1916 .... $8–$10

Box, Amos 'n Andy, Candy, Williamson Candy Co., Chicago–Brooklyn–San Francisco, orange background, ca. 1930 .... $75–$85

Box, Aunt Jemima, pancake flour .... $55–$65

Box, Black Boy, cigar, shows dice, "7 & 11 always win" .... $25–$35

Box, Old Virginia Cheroots, cigar, wood, 1890 .... $35–$55

Box, Pickanninnies, jelly bean, black and orange, 10 lbs. .... $85–$95

Box, Uncle Wabash Cupcakes, cardboard, Schulze Baking Co., copyright 1924 .... $20–$25

Button, Aunt Jemima .... $2–$4

Can, Gold Dust Twins, cleanser, unused .... $10–$14

Can, Old Black Joe, grease, 5 lb. .... $45–$55

Canister, Jumbo Dixie Peanuts, black boy, 10 lb. .... $125–$175

Canister, Luzianne Coffee, pictures Mammy .... $30–$35

Clothes brush, Aunt Jemima .... $6–$8

Comic books, Coca-Cola, Golden Legacy .... $6–$10

Container, Uncle Joe's, cigar .... $25–$35

Counter display figure, Green River Whiskey, composition Negro with horse, rat on saddle .... $175–$200

Coupon, Luzianne Coffee .... $15–$18

Cup, 25 Grain Kaffe, measuring, depicts Negro boy with coffee cup .... $20–$25

Flue cover, black Mammy fortune-teller .... $40–$50

Label, Dixie Boy Fruit, Waverley, Fla., black boy biting grapefruit .... $3–$6

Lunch box, Black Dixie Kid .... $30–$40

Lunch box, Dixie Kid Tobacco, black baby ...... $225–$250

Matchbook, Dinah's Shack .... $10–$15

Menu, Coon Chicken Inn, 12" .... $65–$85

Pail, Aunt Jemima, dated 1928 .... $20–$28

Pail, Luzianne Coffee .... $38–$45

Pail, Mammy's Favorite Coffee, 4 lb. .... $85–$130

Pail, Nigger Hair Tobacco, covered .... $75–$105

Pail, Picanninny Peanut Butter .... $65–$95

Pin, Aunt Jemima, premium .... $1–$3

Placemat, Coon Chicken Inn .... $15–$25

Plate, Coon Chicken Inn, dinner .... $95–$115

Poster, Coca-Cola, black family drinking, 1950s .... $175–$195

Poster, Charles Denby Cigars, black boy with box, stand-up .... $25–$40

Poster, Red Cross Cotton, Negroes picking cotton, 1894 .... $375–$415

Sign, Aunt Jemima, on swing, chromolithograph on tin, 17" .... $32–$45

Sign, Duluth Imperial Flour, black cook, tin, 1910, 18 × 25" .... $625–$775

Sign, Gold Dust Twins, Scrubbin' Tub, dated 1921, 28 × 17" .... $75–$90

Sign, Green River Whiskey, black man and horse, 1899, framed, 42 × 32" .... $875–$980

Sign, Green River Whiskey, old Negro and mule, 1930, paper on board, 28 × 22" .... $75–$95

Sign, Paul Jones Co., Negro woman, huge watermelon, child .... $580–$660

Sign, Temptation of St. Anthony, black farmer with bottle, wife with watermelon, child between, 19½ × 13¾" .... $550–$675

Sign, U.S. Fur Company, black hunter surprised by skunk .... $425–$495

Syrup pitcher, Aunt Jemima, 6" .... $3–$10

Tape measure, Aunt Jemima .... $3–$6

Tieback, Aunt Jemima, hard plastic, set of 6, 1940s .... $20–$35

Tin, Aunt Sally's Candy .... $7–$15

Tin, Benne Bits Cocktail Bits, 10-oz. size, red and white .... $20–$28

Tin, Black Boy Pure Coffee, ½-lb. size, yellow background .... $65–$75

Tin, C.D. Kenny Co., Mammy's Favorite Brand Coffee, 4 lb. .... $55–$80

Tin, Gold Band Roasted Coffee .... $12–$18

Tin, High Brown Face Powder, black girl .... $12–$15

Tin, Lipton Tea, lithograph of black tea pickers, 3 lb. .... $35–$50

Tin, Luzianne Coffee, miniature size, used as sample .... $50–$70

Tin, Luzianne Coffee lady, 1928 .... $35–$40

Tin, Mammy, roly-poly .... $240–$325

Tin, Mammy Coffee, pictures black man .... $75–$130

Tin, Zanzibar brand spices, canister, 1949 .... $15–$20

Tobacco can, nigger hair pail .... $85–$105

Tobacco card, Mayo's, die-cut, with black face .... $10–$15

Toothpick holder, silverplate, New Orleans Centennial Exposition, December 1884 .... $75–$95

Trade cards, 3, Cole and Burt, One Piece Clothiers and Furnishers, 39 Main Street, Bennington, Vermont, color lithographs .... $18–$22

Trays, Romance of Coca-Cola series, pair .... $75–$100

Treasure map, Amos 'n Andy, Pepsodent .... $25–$35

Cardboard store display piece, Schulze Baking Co./Uncle Wabash Cupcakes, copyright 1924. *Courtesy of Jeanie Ohle; photo by Donald Vogt.*

A pair of Coca-Cola trays, part of the Romance of Coca-Cola series, limited editions, numbered and signed "The Courtship" and "The Wedding," ca. 1980. *Courtesy of Malinda Saunders; photo by Donald Vogt.*

Rubber head of black man must have been used in a store window for some kind of advertising because his eyes light up. His hat is not original, but doesn't he wear it jauntily? *Courtesy of Rose Fontanella; photo by Donald Vogt.*

Farm toy, an advertising giveaway for Happy Ham Farm Products of Brandon, Vermont. The wagon is all wood, even the wheels and driver, and some parts are painted. *Courtesy of Rose Fontanella; photo by Donald Vogt.*

2
Art

ON COLLECTING BLACK AMERICAN ART

Collecting art is one of the most widely enjoyed facets of the antique world. Connoisseurs of the arts as well as collectors with smaller checkbooks are able to fill their walls with original art that gives them both visual pleasure and the added bonus of having that piece of art rise in value as time goes by. No matter how little money you have, you can collect art. And, with few exceptions, art is the one thing we can count on increasing in value.

If you decide to collect black American art, you will have many avenues from which to choose. You can accumulate works done strictly by black American artists. Or you can decide to collect paintings/art depicting black Americans. There are black sculptors, painters, and folk artists (we'll get to them in a later chapter) and there are also prints of all the former categories.

For hundreds of years, the black artist's work was much the same as any other artist's of his/her day. There was no distinction, no way to tell whether the artist whose work you were viewing was black, red, white, or yellow.

The black artist, if talented enough, learned under white masters. But no matter how much talent that artist had, the climb to the top of the artistic ladder was extremely rough, and many black artists did not choose to make that climb. Instead, they disappeared from the public's sight or, like the great Henry O. Tanner, took their talents overseas where they could enjoy their art instead of having the attention of their sponsors constantly turned to the color of their skin.

One instance of this racial prejudice that comes to mind is Edward Bannister's experience at the Philadelphia Centennial Exposition in 1876. He had entered his painting *Under the Oaks* and was awarded the bronze medal. However, when the judges discovered the color of his skin, they denied him admission to the gallery where his work was displayed.

It has been said that all art can be judged on two levels: social and artistic. That fact seems to be more blatantly true of Afro-American art than of art by any other American race.

If we attempt to study the routes black American art has taken, we can also follow the political history of that people— the lines are so closely drawn. The influences on black Amer-

Old Couple Looking At Portrait of Lincoln, Henry Ossawa Tanner, oil on canvas, 1892–1893. Part of "Sharing Traditions: Five Black Artists in 19th Century America." *Courtesy of National Museum of American Art; transfer from National Museum of African Art, gift of Norman Robbins.*

ican artists before the Civil War were basically religious. Few, if any, black artists made any other kind of social statement in their paintings. In fact, the black artist before, during, and immediately after the Civil War was more concerned with style, color, and making a living than with angering any white people "kind" enough to pay the price the artist put on his/her work. If the artist were bold enough to include a feeling for the black heritage in his/her work, the reception was usually negative at best.

Because of this attitude toward the black American artist, we have been denied the pleasure of being able to document a large number of early artists. We may never be able to identify those who neglected to sign their works or those whose works have been lost or destroyed.

Until the "Roaring Twenties," the black artist's work went largely unnoticed. A few artists, such as Tanner and Robert Duncanson, were good enough to attain recognition, but for the most part there is no documentation of where, how, and by whom the era of "black art" as a cultural and political tool was started.

BLACK ART HISTORY— A SUMMARY IN DEPTH

EARLY ARTISTS

Although there are paintings and drawings of a style that could be attributed to blacks during the eighteenth century, there is no way to tell who these artists were because most pieces were not signed.

Early Afro-American artists experienced many hardships in their careers. First and foremost was the difficulty of being accepted in the art world; the second was that of trying to preserve their African heritage in such a way that their statements were not overt enough to jeopardize their acceptance.

The "Black Laws" that were enacted shortly after the Civil War—and continued to be enforced, added to, and strengthened for the better part of the century—prohibited black people from settling in certain areas of the country. In some places, blacks had to post a bond in order to assure the white community that they were going to behave in a proper way. Few people of color could raise the price of the bonds, which were as high as $500 in some areas.

During this era blacks concentrated their artistic skills in areas such as silver, sign painting, even ornamental gravestones. The area where slaves seemed to excel the most was in the ironwork and metalwork on mansions throughout the South.

One of the early black artists who was able to surmount the stringent laws of his day was Robert Scott Duncanson (see the biography section of this chapter), who joined the ranks of portrait painters in Cincinnati in 1841, determined to become the greatest landscape painter in America.

Because of his early education in Canada, Duncanson had had opportunities that most American blacks did not. The fact that he grew up in Wilberforce, a town devoted to abolition, meant that young Duncanson emerged well educated and basically untouched by the prejudice so common in American society.

During the 1840s and 1850s, Duncanson was commissioned by wealthy Cincinnati art patrons, traveled widely painting landscapes, and proved himself a noteworthy portraitist.

In the early 1850s, the Anti-Slavery League sponsored Duncanson and William Sonntag, another artist, so that they could travel to Europe to study the masters. As was the case with many other black American artists, Duncanson felt more at home in Europe where the pressure of prejudice was less noticeable.

When he returned to America, Duncanson once more had to deal with slavery and the white versus black issues. The only way he knew how to deal with such volatile issues was to sequester himself in isolated areas where he could paint in peace. He chose to divorce himself from racial problems, and could never quite accept his role in them.

Duncanson's ambition, intelligence, strength, and talent gave rise to a new insight into black American art. The many myths that the American public believed began to dissipate and black American art emerged as a form art patrons were forced to notice. However, the barriers were not totally broken by Duncanson. To this day, the fight for recognition of the black American artist continues.

It is interesting to note, at this point, that a good number of "black American" artists who worked before the turn of the century were not *truly* black Americans. Duncanson was a mulatto, Bannister was born in Nova Scotia, and Edmonia Lewis was half black, half Indian. It is safe to say that at least part of the success of these artists was due to the fact that they were not wholly black.

THE LEGACY OF HENRY TANNER

The black American artist of the nineteenth century who was most deeply affected by the politics of his day appears to have been Henry Ossawa Tanner (1859–1937). Influenced by his religious upbringing—his father was a minister—Tanner was torn by his country's strife and agonized over his need to become an artist. He found it nearly impossible to maintain a career as a black artist in America, and spent a good part of his life in Europe. Tanner was strongly influenced by European styles and artists, as was any artist able to make the trip overseas.

Tanner's painting *The Banjo Lesson*, done in 1863, depicts a grandfatherly black man holding a young boy against his leg. The boy holds a banjo that seems too large for him, and both figures are concentrating on the movement of the boy's hands as they strum the strings. This early work of Tanner's shows, more than his later works, the deepest part of Tanner's psyche. The characters are lifelike and warm; the feeling one gets when looking at the painting is also a warm one. It seems a shame that Tanner could not, or would not, do more paintings of this type. But the world influenced him so deeply that it must have been easier for him to turn to a subject more easily understood and accepted by the American public—biblical scenes.

Although Tanner eventually gained recognition in America, he refused to come back to start a school of Negro art and made it known that he resented being used as a role model for young black artists because he never forgot the prejudice he suffered. Still he never refused young black artists who went to Europe to gain access to his studio.

Tanner left a legacy of masterful paintings and students like William A. Harper, who continued the movement of Negro culture that eventually became known as the "Harlem Renaissance."

THE TWENTIETH CENTURY—BLACK ART COMES OF AGE

Black art followed stilted, imitative styles until after World War I, when paintings produced by black Americans broke the mold. Painters working in this period included Archibald Motley, Palmer Hayden, Malvin Gray Johnson, Laura Wheeler Waring, and W. E. Scott.

In 1915, a center for cultural activities called Karamu House was founded in Cleveland, Ohio. Karamu House produced such talents as Hughie Lee-Smith, Bell Ingrams, Charles Salke, Elmer Brown, William E. Smith, and George Hulsinger.

Before the 1920s, the Art Institute of Chicago accepted black students and was known for turning out a few talented graduates. It was one of the few schools to accept black students before the turn of the century. William A. Harper attended that institution, which helped him, during his short life, to see to the birth of the Negro Renaissance and contribute to the Harmon Exhibitions during the 1920s.

Painters such as William Scott and Edwin A. Harleston came out of this era, asserting themselves, entering the art world painting scenes of black subjects. The trend of black American art was now toward specifically black themes. It was time for black artists to "tell the story," to show intimate, daily views of black Americans on the farm, in the city, at home.

The 1920s was a period of unrest, yet it was a happy time, an era where the black person saw something good could possibly be on its way. Black writers, artists, musicians, and actors came out of this era in large groups. People began to pay attention to the advice and feelings of black leaders. It seemed the black people had given a new definition to "community," and the new community was Harlem

Black art suddenly became modern, colorful, social, and political. Black artists began discovering their roots and proudly displayed these "new" evidences of their African background.

This was a time when white art, music, and writing were also taking a better look at black American life. White photographers, artists, and musicians were busily seeking the secret to portraying black Americans, while writers were producing pieces like *Porgy* and *Emperor Jones*.

In 1928, Archibald Motley was the first Negro artist, other than Tanner, to have a one-man show in New York City. The artists' styles are totally opposite. While Tanner's style follows the classic lines of European painters of his day, Motley's paintings are brightly colored, realistic views of a grotesque side of "modern black life." Motley, active during the 1930s, painted humorous night scenes such as *The Barbecue* and *The Chicken Snack*.

In 1939, the first all-black artists' exhibition was held in the Baltimore Museum. Represented were artists such as Richard Barthe, Malvin Gray Johnson, Henry Bannarn, Florence Purviance, Hale Woodruff, Dox Thrash, Robert Blackburn, and Archibald Motley.

The Depression caused an upheaval in American life which affected black artists and made their earlier achievements of the 1920s seem like an illusion. The country and its citizens, both black and white, were in a deep-blue funk and didn't seem capable of doing anything about it until 1933, when the Public Works of Art Project and the Federal Art Project of the WPA were organized. Artists were now being hired at craftsmen's wages to paint, sculpt, or fix public buildings.

By 1934, old government office buildings had murals, others had drawings, and parks had sculptures. America was finally beginning to pay homage to its artists. It was a profitable way for *any* artists, not just black artists, to support themselves and still not give up their art.

The art of this era is full of social criticism and tends to reflect the poverty the artists were experiencing in a very graphic way. The period is not one in which artists reached great heights, but painters who had done well in the 1920s— Motley, Hayden, Barthe—continued to produce.

Primitive and neo-primitive painting continued to be the style that artists such as Horace Pippin, Leslie Bolling, and William H. Johnson followed. The style is almost abstract in its lines and the portraits are stiff and unrealistic. The black artist continued to paint black life, but the style of putting colors to canvas had changed. It was a sign of growth, a good sign.

During the 1950s and 1960s, black museums and art centers started appearing in major cities all across the United States. And the progress continues, although prominent black artists are still being left out of major museum shows.

In 1985, the Smithsonian Institution's National Museum of American Art put together an exhibition called "Sharing Traditions: Five Black Artists in 19th Century America." The artists exhibited included Henry O. Tanner, Edward Mitchell Bannister, Robert Scott Duncanson, Edmonia Lewis, and Joshua Johnson. It was a major museum showing and an impressive one. Because of that showing and of a deep appreciation for antiques, I have concentrated on those artists and others of their era in this chapter. Mr. Johnson appears in Chapter 7.

Although the ranks of black American artists are swelling every day, there have been few major changes in the American art world. Twenty or thirty years from now we may be able to look back and compare, but now we are too close. In the art world, a little distance sometimes makes all the difference.

Newspaper Boy, Edward Mitchell Bannister, oil on canvas, 1869. Part of "Sharing Traditions: Five Black Artists in 19th Century America." *Courtesy of National Museum of American Art; transfer from National Museum of African Art, gift of Frederick Weingeroff.*

Mount Healthy, Ohio, Robert Scott Duncanson, oil on canvas, 1844. Part of "Sharing Traditions: Five Black Artists in 19th Century America." *Courtesy of National Museum of American Art; transfer from National Museum of African Art, gift of Leonard Granoff.*

THE BLACK AMERICAN ARTIST— SOME BIOGRAPHIES

Edward Mitchell Bannister (1828–1901) was born in St. Andrews, New Brunswick, Canada, and moved to Boston in 1848 to begin his artistic career. He studied with artist and physician William Rimmer at Lowell Institute in the mid-1860s. After graduating, he painted portraits, biblical subjects, seascapes, and landscapes.

Bannister had a little more freedom than earlier black artists and he exercised his need to prove that Negroes had an appreciation of art. When he moved to Providence, Rhode Island, in 1870, he started the Providence Art Club. His painting *Under the Oaks* won a first-place bronze medal at the 1876 Centennial Exposition in Philadelphia, but officials tried to revoke the award when they found out he was black.

Bannister's works include: *Under the Oaks, Sad Memories, Pleasant Pastures, Driving Home the Cows, The Old Ferry, Lady with Bouquet, Sunrise, At Pawtucket, Fort off Jamestown, Sabin Point, Narragansett Bay,* and *After the Storm.*

His work has been exhibited widely in the United States, including at the Rhode Island School of Design, Howard University, the National Center of Afro-American Artists (Boston, 1972), and the Museum of Fine Arts in Boston.

Collections of Bannister's work can be found in the Frederick Douglass Institute of Negro Arts and History in Washington, D.C., the Rhode Island School of Design Museum of Art, and at the New York Public Library in the Schomburg Art Collection.

Bannister died in Providence in 1901.

Richard Barthe was the first Negro sculptor to become a member of the National Headquarters of Arts and Sciences.

Barthe was born in Bay St. Louis, Mississippi, in 1901 and began his training as a painter at the Chicago Art Institute.

His works were bought by the Whitney Museum in New York and his sculpture of Booker T. Washington was placed in New York University's Hall of Fame.

Robert Scott Duncanson (1821–1872) spent most of his childhood in the tolerant atmosphere of Canada, and little is known of his artistic career until he emerged in the art center of Cincinnati in 1841.

As with many other black artists and artisans, he found himself in Europe a number of times during his career, and his landscapes often reflect his knowledge of English, Irish, and Scottish literature. He was more accepted in Europe than in America, where the Civil War still raged. In England, the London press called him the equal of their artists.

His works are included in the National Museum of American Art exhibit "Sharing Traditions: Five Black Artists in 19th Century America."

Meta Vaux Warrick Fuller (1877–1967) was a sculptor, illustrator, and writer. A multitalented woman, Fuller was born in Philadelphia and studied at the Pennsylvania School of Industrial Art from 1899 to 1904, at the Pennsylvania Academy of Fine Arts in 1907, the Academie Colarossi in Paris, and the Ecole des Beaux Arts in Paris.

While in Europe, she studied under a number of well-known sculptors including Rodin, Gauguin, and Raphael Collin and was one of the first black American sculptors to turn away from antislavery pieces.

Fuller's works include: *Water Boy, Procession of Arts and Crafts, Oedipus, Three Gray Women, Swing Along Chillun, Exodus, Mother and Child, The Dancing Girl, Man Carrying a Dead Comrade, The Madonna of Consolation*, and *The Good Samaritan*. She was also known for her busts of famous people. In 1910 a fire in Philadelphia destroyed most of her early works.

Her works have been exhibited all over the world including at the Paris Salon in 1898, 1899, and 1903; at the Boston Art Club in the 1930s; at Howard University in 1961; at the American Negro Exposition; at the Boston Public Library in 1922; at the New York Public Library in 1921; and at City College of New York in 1967.

Fuller belonged to quite a few organizations, among them the Boston Art Club, Zonta (where she was the only Negro chapter president), the American Federation of the Arts, and the Federation of Women's Clubs.

Some of the awards she won during her distinguished career were an honorary degree of Doctor of Letters from Livingston College in 1962, a silver medal for the "New Vistas in American Art" exhibition at Howard University in 1961, and a fellowship at the Academy of Fine Arts.

Parts of her collected works are owned by the Cleveland Art Museum, the Schomburg Collection at the New York Public Library, the Framingham (Massachusetts) Center Library, the San Francisco Museum of Fine Arts, Howard University, and the Business and Professional Women's Club of Washington, D.C.

William Henry Johnson was born in 1901 in Florence, South Carolina. A painter and graphic artist, he studied at the National Academy of Design in New York, under Charles Hawthorne at the Cape Cod School of Art, and in Paris. During 1930–1940 he taught at the Federal Project of the Harlem Art Center.

Some of his works include: *Looking from My Balcony; Flowers to the Teacher; Mother and Child; Study of a Man of Letters; Norway Landscape; Flowering Trees; Three Great Abolitionists, A. Lincoln, F. Douglass and J. Brown*; and *Jitter Bugs VI*.

Johnson painted over seventy works and exhibited at places such as the Harlem Art Center of New York in 1940, various European exhibits during the 1930s, and Howard University and the American Negro Exposition in Chicago in 1940.

He was a member of the United American Artists and won awards such as the Harmon Foundation's gold medal (1930), the Cannon Prize, and the National Academy of Design's Hallgarten Prize.

Leon Lank Leonard, Sr., a prolific painter and sculptor, was born in Waco, Texas, in 1922. He studied at Texas College and the University of Denver School of Art.

His works include: *African Laborer; Negro Statesman, Black Nun; Dr. George Washington Carver; Black Christ*; a marble sculpture entitled *Black Prophet; Three Wise Men*; and *Africa's Black Pilgrimage*.

His work has been exhibited at national art shows including the California State Exposition in Sacramento (1972) and the All-City Outdoor Show in Los Angeles (1969), and at many colleges including Atlanta University (1956–1970), Whittier College, and Dominguez College.

Collections of his work are owned by Atlanta University, Reverend Harold Perry, Mr. Bill Cosby, and Mr. Sugar Ray Robinson.

Leonard was a member of the Texas Watercolor Society, Art West Association North, and the California National Watercolor Society.

Edmonia Lewis was the first black woman sculptor in the United States. Born in Albany, New York, in 1845 of Indian and Negro parentage (her father was a free Negro, her mother a Chippewa Indian), it is not known whether or not Edmonia grew up with her mother's tribe.

William Lloyd Garrison, hearing of her ambition to study art, introduced her to a Boston sculptor named Edmund Brackett who became her mentor.

Lewis studied at Oberlin College as well as training in Brackett's studio in Boston where she specialized in portrait busts and symbolic groups. She was involved in a scandal while at Oberlin when she was accused of poisoning two students. No decision was made on the case because of a lack of evidence.

A bust of John Brown was her first piece. One of her early pieces, a bust of Robert Gould Shave, a Civil War colonel, brought her work to the eyes of Boston's Story family who encouraged her to study in Rome.

While in Rome, she perfected her work with marble and was commissioned by various Europeans and Americans to do work in the neoclassical style. She was looked upon as something of an eccentric and was often visited by people interested in her character and mannerisms. When the neoclassical vogue faded in the 1880s, so did interest in Lewis's work.

Her works include: *Unknown Woman* (1867, marble); *Old Indian Arrow Maker and Daughter* (1872, marble); *Abraham Lincoln; Henry Wadsworth Longfellow; William Lloyd Garrison; Morning of Liberty (Forever Free); Death of Cleopatra*; and busts of Wendell Phillips, Harriet Hosmer, John Brown, and Charles Sumner. Other works include: *Hiawatha, The Marriage of Hiawatha, Hagar in the Wilderness, Madonna and Child*, and a bust of Henry Wadsworth Longfellow that was given to the Harvard College Library.

Her work has been exhibited at the Soldiers Aid Fair in Boston in 1864, the Philadelphia Centennial in 1876, the American Negro Exposition in 1940, the San Francisco Art Association in 1873, Vassar College in 1972, and many shows throughout the United States and Europe. She received commissions from Harvard and many prominent citizens of her day.

Collections of Edmonia Lewis's work are owned by the Frederick Douglass Institute of Negro Arts and History in Washington, D.C., the Harvard College Library, and the

Kennedy Gallery in New York City.

Lewis died in Rome, in obscurity, in 1890.

Scipio Morehead is the only eighteenth-century black artist to have been recorded in colonial America. He was aided by two prominent Bostonian women, one a patron of the arts and the other the black poet Phyllis Wheatley.

Henry Ossawa Tanner was born in 1859 in Pittsburgh, Pennsylvania, the son of an A.M.E. Church bishop named Benjamin Tucker Tanner. Henry was expected to follow in his father's footsteps, but he preferred art, thus causing an upset in his family. In spite of his family's protests, he entered the Pennsylvania Academy of Fine Arts and studied under Thomas Eakins and William Chase.

When he wanted to study in Europe after graduation, his family sent him to Atlanta to visit his brother who was a pastor there. While there, he became a photographer and chose to make his living teaching art at Clark University and selling his paintings and photographs. During his time in Atlanta, Tanner experienced quite a bit of prejudice and began dreaming of making a move to Paris where artists were valued no matter what their color.

A meeting with Bishop Hartzell led to an exhibit of Tanner's work being arranged in Cincinnati. Tanner hoped he could sell enough paintings to finance his trip to Europe. When no sales were made, Hartzell bought the whole collection and, through further efforts, made it possible for Tanner to study in Paris.

Thus, in 1892, Tanner became a student at the Académie Julian, studying under Benjamin Constant and Paul Laurens. Four years later, his paintings *Music Lesson* and *Young Sabot-Maker* were noticed and his career went on the upswing.

Tanner painted Southern blacks and French peasants while living in France, but his major concentration was on religious themes. During his life abroad, he visited such places as Egypt, Palestine, and Morocco, often reflecting what he saw there in his paintings. His painting *The Resurrection of Lazarus* won him recognition as a great artist in 1897 and the work was sold to the Luxembourg Gallery.

After visiting Palestine, Tanner did a series of biblical paintings that further secured his fame and fortune. Paintings from this era of his career hang in prominent American museums.

In 1900 Tanner received the Lippincott Prize, the silver medal at the Paris Exposition, the gold medal at the San Francisco Exposition, and the French Legion of Honor. He resented the American way of publicizing his race instead of his talent and, because of that fact, remained in Paris until his death.

Tanner was a prolific painter, producing over a hundred works in his career. The majority of his paintings deal with religious subjects, such as *Destruction of Sodom and Gomorrah, Flight from Egypt, Moses and the Burning Bush, Christ at the Home of Mary and Martha, Study for Christ,* and *Nicodemus on a Rooftop,* as well as many others.

His work hangs in major museums of the world and has been exhibited in France and the United States many times. Collections/pieces of his work hang in the Louvre in Paris, the

Old Arrow Maker, Edmonia Lewis, marble, ca. 1872. Part of "Sharing Traditions: Five Black Artists in 19th Century America." *Courtesy of National Museum of American Art; transfer from National Museum of African Art, gift of Norman Robbins.*

Carnegie Institute in Pittsburgh, the Frederick Douglass Institute in Washington, D.C., the Houston Museum of Fine Arts, the Howard University Gallery of Art, the Metropolitan Museum of Art, and the New York Public Library's Schomburg Collection.

Tanner was awarded many honors in Paris around the turn of the century, and won the National Arts Club bronze medal at the Exhibition of Arts Club Galleries in New York in 1927.

He was a member of many organizations including the Legion of Honor, an associate at the National Academician, and a member of the Paris Society of American Painters (1909) and the American Artists Professional League.

Most significant among Tanner's accomplishments is that he was the first black American artist to live solely from his art.

OTHER ARTISTS WHO PAINTED BLACK SUBJECTS

Theresa Bernstein was born in Philadelphia and received her art training at the Philadelphia School of Design and the Pennsylvania Academy. She moved to New York City in 1910 where she proceeded to establish her reputation as an independent-minded "modern realist."

Choosing her subject matter from the New York streets, she painted in the "ashcan" tradition while developing and maintaining her own style.

In 1983 Bernstein and her husband, the artist William Meyerowitz, were given an exhibition at the New York Historical Society. It was the first time that institution had had a show by a living artist.

Bernstein's work is in many museum collections including the Corcoran Gallery, the Metropolitan Museum, the Brooklyn Museum, and the Chicago Art Institute.

Eleazer Hutchinson Miller, born in Shepherdstown, West Virginia, in 1831, lived most of his life in Washington, D.C. He worked as painter, illustrator, and etcher, producing work for both periodicals and books such as the illustrations for *Tam O'Shanter* and Mrs. Springer's *Songs of the Sea*.

Miller's etching skills gained him entrance into the prestigious New York Etchers' Club. He was also a founding member of the Washington Art Club and the Society of Washington Artists.

While living in Washington, Miller worked for the *National Intelligencer*. In 1859 he married Mary Farnham and took her with him to Europe in 1875, where he studied the old masters. He died in Washington in 1921.

Edward H. Potthast was born in Cincinnati in 1857. He studied there as well as in Munich and Paris. In 1906 he was elected a member of the National Academy. In addition to his fame as a fine art painter, he was also a well-known illustrator for both *Scribner's* and *Century* magazines. His work is represented in major collections such as the Cincinnati Art Museum, the Brooklyn Museum, and the Buffalo Museum.

Frederic Remington, the well-known artist who is best known for his illustrations of the Old West, drew black cavalry troopers while working for *Harper's Weekly* in 1888.

Agnes M. Richmond was born about 1870 in Alton, Illinois, and educated at the St. Louis School of Fine Arts. In 1888 she went to New York City to study at the Art Students League and studied with John Henry Twachtmann, Walter Appleton Clark, and Kenyon Cox. She taught at the League from 1910 to 1914.

Richmond won many prizes during her career, including the Watrous Figure Prize. She was also a member of many art organizations, and had her work exhibited at the Smithsonian, the Carnegie Institute, the Art Association at Newport, the Brooklyn Museum, the San Diego Fine Arts Society, and the Hickory North Carolina Museum of Art, among others.

Richmond also served on juries of selection and award along with other notable women artists of her day. The *Woman's Who's Who of America* (1914–1915) notes that she was "interested in socialism, favors woman's suffrage . . ." She died in Brooklyn in 1964.

Harry Roseland was born in Brooklyn in 1867. He studied in New York with Beckwith and was a member of the Brooklyn Art Club.

Roseland painted scenes of later nineteenth-century well-heeled white women with black women of the same age. Often the women were involved in a card or tea reading or seemed to be sharing some kind of knowledge. The paintings are romantically done with both subjects seeming to be more beautiful in oil than they would be in reality.

William Aiken Walker (1838–1921) lived in Charleston, Baltimore, New Orleans, and other cities in the deep South. He was largely self-taught although he spent time during the 1860s studying in Dusseldorf, Germany. In 1888, Currier and Ives published two of his lithographs. Walker preferred to paint rural blacks at work, on docks, in fields, and at home. His style approached that of folk art.

Early in 1985 Sotheby's sold a William Aiken Walker painting entitled *Newsboy* for $23,100. (The pre-auction estimate had been $5,000 to $7,000.) It was said that the painting generated more interest than Walker's usual cabin scenes and cotton pickers because the subject was an unusual one. During the same period, a Phillips auction brought out one of Walker's more common subjects, a cabin scene, and it was knocked down for $5,500 (pre-auction estimate $4,000–6,000).

PRICE GUIDE—ART

It is difficult to give an art price guide because the prices of art change so much more rapidly than those of antiques and collectibles. Buyers should be prepared to pay whatever is comfortable for them for a piece of art they will enjoy. You should also be aware of popularity trends and of what an artist's paintings have brought in the past—paintings by Edward Mitchell Bannister, for example, usually fetch a four-figure sum. In other words, educate thyself!

Don't be afraid to hesitate before buying an expensive painting, sculpture, bronze, or print. Back off from the painting, think about your purchase, and, if necessary, wait a day or two so that you can do the proper research before emptying out your bank account. If you buy wisely, you'll never be sorry. If you don't, you can sing the song of foolishness right along with the rest of us "experts," because making mistakes is just another accepted aspect of collecting.

Buying art done by or depicting black Americans is different from buying a more specific art—for example, the Hudson River School or the works of Picasso—because you have such a wide variety of choices available to you. Black art can be abstract or realistic, reminiscent of the Renaissance or of a style totally its own. Black art is marble and clay, oil and crayon, canvas and wood. The artists who were not black, yet painted black subjects, are as varied as the styles of black art. Some paintings are complimentary, even ethereal. Some are so realistic that it wrenches the heart out of your chest. Some make you want to laugh, some to weep.

Abraham's Oak, Henry Ossawa Tanner, oil on canvas, 1905. Part of "Sharing Traditions: Five Black Artists in 19th Century America." *Courtesy of National Museum of American Art; transfer from National Museum of African Art, gift of Norman Robbins.*

Star Gazer, Edward H. Potthast, pen, ink, and gouache on paper, signed lower left. *Photo courtesy of Jeffrey Alan Gallery.*

Selling Christmas Greens, Eleazer Hutchinson Miller, oil on canvas, signed and dated 1901. *Photo courtesy of Jeffrey Alan Gallery.*

Black Church Wedding, Theresa Bernstein, oil on canvas, signed lower right-hand corner. *Photo courtesy of Jeffrey Alan Gallery.*

19

Beulah, Agnes M. Richmond, oil on canvas, signed and dated 1925, upper right-hand corner. *Photo courtesy of Jeffrey Alan Gallery.*

Pencil drawing of slave on back of sheet music, ca. 1850, attributed to William Aiken Walker, unsigned. *Collection of Joseph W. and Nathan Wood; photo by Donald Vogt.*

Chalkware bust, signed C. Morrett, copyright 1889. The girl with the ruffled hat has a "brother" also signed and dated by Morrett. The sculptures are highly colorful and stand well over a foot tall. *Courtesy of Thomas Evan Robinson; photo by Donald Vogt.*

You cannot expect to get a "bargain" when a painting with a black subject is offered for sale. However, when buying the work of a black artist, you may be able to pick up expensive paintings for a song. Again, education is the key.

For those who just *have* to know, I have researched some of the major artists and below is my approximation of their worth. Again, new records are being made every day, so these prices should not be taken as stable and permanent.

Chalkware sculpture of three boys eating watermelon copyright 1898, done by J. Nardi, a Boston artist who worked in the latter part of the nineteenth century. Nardi specialized in sculptures of black people accompanied by chickens and/or watermelons. *Courtesy of Thomas Evan Robinson; photo by Donald Vogt.*

• *Bannister, Edward M.*—Recent prices for paintings by this Renaissance-type artist range from the lower thousands to the mid and upper teens. It is imaginable that his paintings would bring quite a bit more if his better works were being sold. His best pieces are held by museums and in private collections.

• *Roseland, Harry*—Roseland's prints often receive between $90 and $175 while his paintings have run the gamut from $500 to $15,000. Often his subjects are what makes the price of his paintings. His romanticized characters are attractive, the subjects well illustrated and often touching. His use of black "fortune-tellers" is well known. The scenes are often populated by obviously well-to-do white ladies along with the "mammy" caricature of the black woman. Yet one gets the feeling when looking at his depiction that the black woman is more knowledgeable in areas that the higher-class white woman envies, such as being able to predict the future. Roseland prints are usually found in any general collection of black Americana.

• *Tanner, Henry Ossawa*—When I think of Tanner, I see him as a rather scholarly gentleman, a man with deep feelings and conviction, both sensitive and intelligent. Pictures often show him with glasses on the bridge of his nose, looking more the college professor than the traveling artist. Tanner's works hang in major museums throughout the world. He is one of the best known of the early black artists and his work is highly acclaimed and expensive, with average prices in the neighborhood of $250,000.

• *Walker, William Aiken*—Walker's works are well known for the Southern scenes they depict. His paintings of cotton pickers and slave life have even been reproduced in a series of bisque dolls. His paintings run from $4,000 to somewhere in the mid-teens. His rich colors and poignant renditions of life on the plantation have attracted many collectors and I expect you will see this painter's worth climb even higher.

Should you want to find out the value of a particular artist, your local library will have a number of volumes to help you. The one most art dealers and antique dealers use is *Jacobsen's Price Guide.* For finding the history of a particular artist, *Fielding's* gives a concise and accurate listing of each artist. Other, more specialized books are also available to help you in your search.

ON COLLECTING PRINTS

Many prints have been made of black subjects. Some were initially made to be just that: prints. Others were reprints of a particular piece of art—such as Harry Roseland's paintings.

Prints can be divided into many categories. There are chromolithographs, lithographs, first edition prints, numbered prints, and so on. To make it easy, chromolithographs are colored prints produced by lithography. Lithographs are produced by making a "picture" on a stone or metal plate and transferring it to a material that will accept ink.

As in all areas of black Americana, there are many avenues to choose from when collecting prints. One can stick strictly to Currier and Ives, or to Roseland prints, or Audubons. Or one may choose to collect Raphael Tuck's greeting cards, postcards, or prints. You are the collector. You know what you like. And what you like is what you should collect.

It is interesting to note that during the 1870s and 1880s, quite a few black artists made their living as lithographers and engravers. Grafton T. Brown is one of the more notable (see biography below).

Other printmakers who made a number of black prints were not black themselves, but are included here because of their great impact on the antiques world—for example, Currier and Ives.

PRINT BIOGRAPHIES

John J. Audubon was born to Pierre Audubon, a wealthy, society Frenchman, and Jeanne Rabine, Audubon's mulatto servant, on April 26, 1785, in Haiti. The parents were not married, but the child was adopted by Audubon and his wife. They brought their adopted son with them to France, where he studied with Jacques-Louis David before moving to America in 1803. Audubon was treated and brought up as a white Frenchman.

Audubon spent his life traveling and studying nature, animals, and birds until his health and age no longer permitted him to spend long periods of time in the woods. His nature prints are widely collected and quite valuable in today's antiques market. There are few people who realize that Audubon's ancestry was black.

Grafton T. Brown made his living as a draftsman, painter, and lithographer. He worked in a seminaturalistic style, picturing geographic locations so that they were recognizable.

Brown spent most of his career in San Francisco and it was there that he opened his own lithographic business in 1867. During the last fifty years of his life, Brown became involved in engineering and geological science. He died in 1918 in St. Paul, Minnesota.

Currier and Ives. Nathaniel Currier began his print business in 1834. Currier, who perfected the art of hand-coloring black-and-white stone lithographs, was joined by James Merritt Ives in 1852. They printed political and humorous prints as well as becoming adept at depicting the major historical events in American life. At times they were inaccurate, but they printed what they believed to be the truth. There were well over 7,000 individual prints published and no records were kept on how many copies of each print were made.

Currier and Ives used artists such as Fanny F. Palmer, Charles Parsons, James E. Butterworth, Louis Maurer, George Catlin, A. F. Tait, George Henry Durrie, and Thomas Worth.

Currier and Ives began to get away from depicting the black American as a bumbling "darky" during the Civil War period. The Negro began to be depicted as a valiant soldier, part of a courageous unit that fought the famous battle of July 18, 1863, losing Robert Shaw, colonel of the 54th Regiment, a totally black unit.

Although the scenes of the Mississippi are interesting and uplifting, for the most part they are inaccurate images of the way life was lived on that river highway. However, Currier and Ives were working to supply a demand and showed Americans views of a new way of life that was then foreign to most natives.

Dedicated English outdoorsman Arthur Fitzwilliam Tait's sketches of the American wilderness were bought by Currier and Ives to appeal to ordinary male Americans caught up in hunting and fishing. The prints, on the market after 1850, sold well and were fairly accurate.

Louis Prang's chromolithograph factory in Boston produced his prints over several decades in the latter part of the nineteenth century. They were so popular that *The American Women's Home*, written by Catherine E. Beecher and Harriet Beecher Stowe, recommended that people decorate their homes with Prang's chromolithographs.

One Prang chromo, entitled *The Old Kentucky Home* (after E. Johnson), shows the back of a house where various members of a black family are playing and talking. Other Prang chromos depict black American life in a more or less romantic fashion.

In 1890, Prang began producing greeting cards and postcards.

Patrick H. Reason was a free mulatto whose engravings and lithographs in support of abolition were widely distributed. He actively applied his art in support of antislavery causes in the early nineteenth century, speaking out against slavery whenever possible and devoting much of his time to illustrating abolitionist literature.

Henry Bibb, who wrote *The American Slave*, sat for Reason and shared some of Reason's beliefs.

PRICE GUIDE—PRINTS

ARTIST/DESCRIPTION   APPROXIMATE PRICE

Audubon, *Black Tailed Deer,* in frame $1,200

Audubon, *Buntings and Finches* $1,350

Audubon, *Hare Indian Dog,* in frame $1,450

Currier and Ives, *American Jockey Club Races, Jerome Park* $850

Currier and Ives, *O Dat Watermillon* $250

Currier and Ives, *Drawing Fust Blood,* Darky Series, 1882 .... $260

Prang, *The Old Kentucky Home* $85

Roseland, *The Fortune Teller* $125

THE DARKTOWN FIRE BRIGADE - SAVED!

Saved!, from Currier and Ives's Darktown Fire Brigade series. Copyright 1884. *Courtesy of Rose Fontanella; photo by Donald Vogt.*

Woodcut of a hanging (print) by WPA artist Elizabeth Catlett. *Courtesy of Rose Fontanella; photo by Donald Vogt.*

Woodcut of Harriet Tubman (print) leading her people. By WPA artist Elizabeth Catlett, dated 1946, signed by the artist. *Courtesy of Rose Fontanella; photo by Donald Vogt.*

3

Banks

In almost every collection of black items, one is sure to find a still or mechanical bank that depicts black people as they were seen in the late 1800s. The days after the Civil War found much of the country angry about the black man's newfound freedom, yet not able to do much about it. Still, the bigotry, prejudice, and racial tension crept into everyday living and reflected the fact that white America had not yet accepted their fellow black countrymen.

The Freedman's Bank, for example, was a political anti-Negro comment on freed black men's behavior after the Civil War. The bank shows a black bank teller taking money while thumbing his nose.

A BRIEF HISTORY OF BANKS

Banks have been found in most ancient cultures, but most had a different purpose than our piggy banks. Some were used to hold offerings for gods, some held the goods of deceased people.

The first iron banks were stills, but once the simple spring action brought life to a bank, more and more intricate movements became popular, causing a peak in mechanical bank sales to be reached before the end of the century.

Cast-iron mechanical banks are purely American products. It seems that ingenious Americans, with their love for competitive, capitalistic culture, wanted a more interesting way to save those pennies, dimes, and nickels.

Banks produced in the years after the Civil War reflect the social, political, and cultural views of the times. They show historical events as well as predictions of technological advances. The height of popularity of mechanical banks spans a sixty-year period from 1870 to 1930.

Some of the companies that produced ethnic versions of mechanical and still banks are listed below. It should be noted, however, that most companies did not mark their banks. Unless you know which companies produced certain banks, you will have a hard time attributing the right maker to the right bank. There are several very good books on the market that can point you in the right direction.

J. & E. Stevens of Cromwell, Connecticut, was the most prolific of the bank manufacturers, producing the first me-

chanical bank and many others after that, working over a period of fifty years. They began manufacturing still banks during the late 1860s and ceased producing all types of banks in 1928. Some of the ethnic banks produced by this prolific firm are among the most popular and most recognized by collectors in this field. "Bad Accident," "Dentist," "Darktown Battery," "I Always Did 'Spise a Mule," "Jolly Nigger," and "Horse Race" are some of them.

Weeden Manufacturing Company of New Bedford, Massachusetts, produced tin windup mechanical banks such as Weeden's Plantation. The company, known for its toy steam engines, began producing tin mechanicals in the late 1880s. Though Weeden's Plantation is fairly easy to find, often the figure of the dancer on the left side of the cabin is missing.

Jerome B. Secor of Bridgeport, Connecticut, manufactured the most valuable mechanical bank of all time, the striking Freedman's Bank. It was the only bank made by Secor and is thought to have been made for only five years (1878–1883). The bank is advertised in an 1880 circular for sale for $4.50—expensive even then. Because only a few of these banks are still available, they are extremely valuable. Prices of $100,000 and up have been reported. A full-page color photo of the bank is shown in Carole Rogers's book *Penny Banks: A History and a Handbook.*

Shephard Hardware Manufacturing Company of Buffalo and *Rex Kyser and Rex* of Philadelphia were other early bank manufacturers.

Charles A. Bailey is the bank designer whose name one sees most often. He was responsible for at least twenty-nine designs, but his banks are difficult to find nowadays because of the fragile spring mechanism favored by Bailey.

Ethnic bias began cropping up in the bank manufacturing circles from 1860 on. Blacks were not the only ones against whom white Americans were prejudiced. The Chinese, Irish, and Jews were also attacked. Banks were made depicting Chinese as sneaky thieves, Irishmen with pigs, and Jews as greedy businessmen. But the blacks were by far the most stereotyped. There are ten versions of the bust bank, all with the stereotypical big lips, large, bulging eyes, and kinky hair. And there are more than twenty other mechanical banks always portraying black people as the butt of some obvious joke. The bank "Bad Accident" depicts the black farmer as ignorant and slow.

Cabin bank made of cast iron, possibly by Stevens Co. *Courtesy of Jim Bollman, The Music Emporium; photo by Donald Vogt.*

Cast-iron still banks depicting a sharecropper and his wife. Approximately 5″ tall. *Courtesy of Jan Thalberg; photo by Donald Vogt.*

Two mechanical bust banks, Dinah and Joe. Hand inserts money into mouth. *Courtesy of Frank Morse Collection; photo by Donald Vogt.*

However, one bank called "Darktown Battery," designed by James Bowen and manufactured by the Stevens Company, shows three black baseball players and makes no derogatory comment on the black race. Ironically, this bank was made before black baseball players were allowed to participate in the major leagues!

COLLECTIBLE BLACK BANKS—SOME DESCRIPTIONS

• *Bad Accident*, manufactured by J. & E. Stevens Company during the 1890s, is 6" tall. A black man sits in a cart drawn by a mule. Behind a bush hides a black boy who, after the coin is dropped between the driver's feet, darts in front of the donkey causing it to rear, the driver to tilt back, and the coin to drop into the bottom of the cart. The words "Bad Accident" are printed on the base, facing the back of the bank. Should you find this bank with the letters facing the front of the bank, you have found a rare version.

• *Darktown Battery*, manufactured by the J. & E. Stevens Company, is 7¼" tall. The bank shows three black baseball players: pitcher, hitter, and catcher. After the coin is placed in the pitcher's hand, a lever is pressed behind the catcher. The pitcher pitches the ball, the hitter turns his head to watch it go by, the catcher catches the ball, the coin enters the catcher's body and is deposited into the bank. The bank is unusual because all three figures have movable parts. The words "Darktown Battery" appear on the base of the bank.

• *Darky Fisherman*, attributed to Charles A. Bailey of Cobalt, Connecticut, was made in the 1880s and is 4¼" tall. It is an extremely rare lead bank. At the base of the bank, near the boy's feet, are the words "Dis Pond Am De Boss Place to Fish." The boy stands at one end of the bank, holding a fishing pole with a fish on its end. When a coin is placed in the slot in the "pond" and a lever at the boy's right elbow is pressed, the fish emerges and pushes the penny into the bank.

• *Dentist*, manufactured by the J. & E. Stevens Company in the 1880s, is 6½" tall. The bank features a black man who is seated in the dentist's chair. The dentist, who is white and sports a large moustache, is bent over his patient. When a coin is placed in the dentist's pocket and a lever pressed next to his foot, the tooth is extracted, the dentist falls back, the patient topples off his chair, and the penny slides into the gas bag behind the dentist.

• *Freedman's Bank*, manufactured by Jerome Secor of Bridgeport, Connecticut, is 10¾" high. One of the most beautiful, as well as rarest, of all mechanicals, the bank is made out of wood, cloth, and metal. It features a black man with a wide smile, dressed in a flowered outfit resembling a clown's, complete with red bow tie and starched collar. He stands behind a wooden box on turned legs. On the front of the box is a plate marked "Freedman's Bank."

The bank must first be wound, then a coin placed on the table and a lever on the side of the bank pressed. The man's left hand slides the coin into the opening. His right hand raises to thumb his nose at the viewer as he simultaneously nods his head.

• *Horse Race*, manufactured by J. & E. Stevens Company, is 4¾" tall. The bank shows a circular platform with two archways, one on each end of the platform. A black man in short blue pants stands in the middle of the circle next to a raised slot. When the coin is dropped into the slot, the horses begin to revolve around the platform. The base of the bank is yellow and orange, one horse is white and the other is brown. This bank was made in two versions, the one described and another, taller and with a coin trap in the bottom.

• *"I Always Did 'Spise a Mule,"* manufactured by J. & E. Stevens Company, was patented April 22, 1879, and April 27, 1897. There were two versions of this bank. The earlier one showed a rider being tossed from a kicking mule. The latter, and more common, version shows a black man seated on the ground in front of what appears to be a very reluctant mule. When the coin is placed on the tray beneath the figure, the mule spins around and kicks over the black man. When the man falls, the coin is deposited into the bank.

• *Jolly Nigger*, manufactured by Shephard Hardware Company and J. & E. Stevens Company, was patented November 14, 1882, and is 6¾" tall. This mechanical bust was the only American-made "Jolly Nigger." A plate on the back of the bank shows the patent date. The bank depicts an exaggerated black man's face. The man wears a red shirt. When a coin is placed in his hand, the arm lifts to deposit the coin in his mouth and his eyes roll.

• *Weeden's Plantation* was manufactured by the Weeden Manufacturing Company in New Bedford, Massachusetts, and stands 5½" tall. Construction of the bank is tin and wood with a clockwork mechanism. The bank looks like a small shack. In front of the shack sits a black banjo player on the right with a black dancer on the left. "Jig Dancin' " is written on one side of the shed and on the other is written "Pete Jones, Banjo Lessuns, One Cent." The mechanism is wound with a key, the coin is inserted at the side of the shack, and the banjo player and dancer perform.

REPRODUCTION BANKS

From about 1870 until World War I, banks were made of heavy cast metal with bright enamel painting, and came in hundreds of styles. Most of the popular ones, mechanical as well as still, have been reproduced and the buyer should beware. Because of the popularity and rarity of the black-oriented models, the price range may vary from state to state.

One of the best ways to spot a repro bank is by being familiar with old banks first. Look at the old banks, feel the smoothness of the paint, note the places where wear is usually most evident. Note how the pieces of the bank fit together—old banks fit together well; repros are often loose. Check the screws. Old screws often have the line in the middle slightly off

Mechanical bank, a later version of "Always Did 'Spise a Mule," James H. Bowen Co. *Courtesy of Frank Morse Collection; photo by Donald Vogt.*

center. New screws are obviously shiny. The color of the paint on new banks is bright. Old paint has a definite "look" to it.

Take the time to study what banks are available and the prices of the items you are attracted to. Take the time, also, to study the reproduced banks. Before buying, know your market.

Banks that have been repaired and repainted are often put up for sale. Though one cannot always buy banks in excellent condition, it is wise to be able to tell whether parts are missing, replacement parts have been made, or the old paint has been redone.

Other defects to watch for include fakes, variations, or pattern banks. Fakes were never banks to begin with. Variations may have the body of one bank with the parts of another. And pattern banks, using original pieces from the old foundries to make new banks, are extremely rare.

The best defense against any and all of these incongruities is to know what you are buying before you buy. Most dealers are eager to share their knowledge with beginning collectors and there are many informative books, as well as collector's clubs, that could educate the most dedicated collector.

PRICE GUIDE—BANKS

MECHANICAL BANKS

DESCRIPTION   APPROXIMATE PRICE

"Always Did 'Spise a Mule," J. & E. Stevens Co.,
8¼", missing trap door, 19th century .... $250–$275
Same bank, in mint condition .... $350–$475
Black mammy, feeding dish .... $350–$400
Black man in cabin .... $225–$275
Black minstrel, original paint, tin .... $185–$215
Book of Knowledge, black man riding mule,
1950s .... $70–$90
Boys stealing watermelon, cast iron .... $4,000–$5,000
Darktown Battery, J. & E. Stevens Co., 7¼",
19th century .... $650–$795

Dinah .... $280–$335
High Hat, black man .... $600–$675
Jolly black man, tin, c. 1955 .... $25–$65
Jolly black man with top hat .... $375–$450
Jolly Nigger, cast iron .... $150–$240
Mammy bank, cast iron, ca. 1888, triple animation,
one coin goes in spoon, one in Mammy's
apron; head goes back and forth, spoon
pushes corn into baby's mouth, and
baby's feet lift .... $2,250–$3,500
Sharecropper, cast iron .... $20–$65
Stump Speaker, black man drops coin into
suitcase .... $1,250–$1,500
Two-faced Negro, cast iron, 3" .... $80–$100
Uncle Remus .... $1,000–$1,200
Uncle Tom, cast iron, 5½" .... $150–$200
Weeden's Plantation, two black men on stage,
one with banjo, other dancing .... $450–$600

STILL BANKS

Aunt Jemima, cast iron .... $40–$68
Baby in cradle, cast iron, 3⅞" .... $925–$1,000
Black boy head, double-faced, cast iron .... $140–$175
Black boy, nodder, eating watermelon, souvenir,
Biloxi .... $50–$80
Black boy, plaster .... $15–$25
Black double face, silver paint, cast iron, 4" .... $60–$80
Black face with turban, pottery .... $25–$45
Black man on slide, cast iron, 6" .... $35–$45
Black man, wooden base, cast iron .... $65–$80
Black sharecropper, cast iron .... $90–$125
Dime Register, Jackie Robinson, tin, 2" .... $58–$75
Lucky Joe, glass .... $14–$20
Mammy, cast iron .... $60–$70
Mammy with spoon, cast iron, 8" .... $95–$105

THE HISTORY

OF

SLAVERY AND THE SLAVE TRADE,

ANCIENT AND MODERN.

THE FORMS OF SLAVERY THAT PREVAILED IN ANCIENT NATIONS,
PARTICULARLY IN GREECE AND ROME.

THE AFRICAN SLAVE TRADE

AND THE

POLITICAL HISTORY OF SLAVERY

IN THE

UNITED STATES.

COMPILED FROM AUTHENTIC MATERIALS
BY W. O. BLAKE.

COLUMBUS, OHIO:
PUBLISHED AND SOLD EXCLUSIVELY BY SUBSCRIPTION
BY J. & H. MILLER.

4

Books

BOOKS BY AND ABOUT THE BLACK AMERICAN

As with other fields of black Americana, with books you have a choice of limiting your collection to published works by black authors or you can extend your area of interest to include works written about black Americans. The latter category includes black writers as well as writers of other races. You can further narrow your scope by collecting only children's books, or perhaps first editions. Whatever your pleasure, you are in great company because just about everyone, at one time or another, has had a collection of books.

Perhaps the most important thing to realize about collecting books by or about black Americans is that you may often become frustrated by the lack of information about the author and/or the subject. Research departments in libraries can be of great assistance.

You can also expect prices on books by and about black Americans to shoot up even more than they already have. Book collectors have been aware of the value of this type of book for many years.

Often books by black writers were not published in quantity. Even more often, there was never more than one edition of such a book.

When you examine the brief history of black writers that I have included later in this chapter, you may further understand why there are so few books available to the public that were written by black people.

One could confine the search to include only books written by contemporary black authors, or to those authors who wrote autobiographies or slave narratives. Whatever group of writers whose works you intend to collect, your first and most important step is to familiarize yourself with the author's biography and to get a listing of his/her works. From there, the search is on. And you begin learning much more than you could ever anticipate.

The black writers are the part of the Negro race who held the most secrets, exposed the most truths (and lies), and asked the most questions. It is they who took chances breaking into new fields and, although most met with little, or some hard-earned,

success, they were most responsible for opening new doors—and minds.

Children's illustrated books such as *Little Black Sambo* or *Uncle Tom's Cabin*, when found in mint condition, can be quite expensive. For some time now, collectors of childhood items have known the value of illustrated children's books that feature blacks as their main characters. If the book was printed in the mid-1800s to early 1900s, you can count on having a treasure. After that time, the paper was of a lesser quality and the illustrations often not quite as bright or as intricately drawn.

Characters like Little Black Sambo underwent many changes during their literary lives. Books of that type were published many times by many different publishers, and the quality of each edition is unique. The characters may even change in appearance and sometimes may seem to have acquired a totally different personality.

When one thinks of the story line of *Little Black Sambo*, it comes as no surprise that many children who grew up reading such "bedtime stories" became prejudiced adults. It is the most blatantly subtle form of hypnosis. Some parents may deny teaching their child bigotry, yet if their reading material were examined, often we would find that the child was being taught certain values from the first moment Mommy or Daddy picked up a picture book and began to read aloud.

BLACK AUTHORS

SLAVE NARRATIVES

Poignant and provocative, slave narratives are a starting point when studying black prose. The tradition seen in later black writers' works appears to have started here. Writers such as Marion Wilson Starling, Charles H. Nichols, Richard Wright, Ralph Ellison, and James Baldwin have written effectively on the subject of the slave narrative.

The first slave narrative appeared in Boston in 1760 and was titled A *Narrative of the Uncommon Sufferings and Surprising Deliverance of Briton Hammon, A Negro Man.*

Jupiter Hammon wrote *An Address to the Negroes in the State of New York*, which reflected his favored position as the literate slave of a Long Island master.

After the works of Hammon and of Phyllis Wheatley, the first black American poetess, were published, legal restrictions

(Facing)
Title page of *The History of Slavery and the Slave Trade*, copyright 1857. *Courtesy of Valerie Bertrand Collection; photo by Donald Vogt.*

were placed on the education of slaves in the American colonies. The government wanted to control the slaves, to keep them from spreading slave news and propaganda that would incite a lust for freedom. Thus, slave poetry went underground for a while and was released verbally in songs instead of via the written word.

Other slave narratives, such as *Scenes in the Life of Harriet Tubman* and *Memoirs of Eleanor Eldridge* (1838), were presented as autobiographies. Some were "told-to" accounts, such as *The Confession of Nat Turner* (1831) and *The Narrative of James Williams* (1838) as dictated to John Greenleaf Whittier.

One of the best-known and most influential of all slave narratives is *Narrative of the Life of Frederick Douglass, An American Slave, Written by Himself* (Boston, 1845). He wrote the book in 1844, less than five years after he ran away from slavery (see Douglass's biography later in this chapter).

By the late 1850s, the slave narrative was in vogue with the literary public. Hundreds of narratives were published during that time.

Decades elapsed between 1859 and the publication of works by Paul Laurence Dunbar and Charles Waddell Chesnutt. However, slave narratives did not end abruptly. Old versions, such as Douglass's, continued to be reissued and over the years new ones continued to appear. *Up from Slavery, An Autobiography*, by Booker T. Washington, was written in 1900 and is considered to be a classic example of the American success story.

AFTER THE TURN OF THE CENTURY

The first Negro newspaper was published in 1927. It was called *Freedom's Journal*, and its first issue contained an abolitionist editorial. The first Negro graduate of Bowdoin College, John Russworm, and Samuel Cornish were the original founders of the paper.

After the Great Depression, black writers were scattered and defeated. It took a while before the black writing community produced such luminaries as Richard Wright, Ralph Ellison, and Frank Yerby.

A new era was then ushered in on the shirttails of Wright's and Ellison's fame. A period of rebellion or revolution began in the black community and young black writers were the first to benefit. The Harlem Renaissance had begun.

The Harlem period is notable because its poets appeared in groups. Since that time, black American poets have appeared in procession and the line remains unbroken. Poets such as Margaret Walker ("For My People," 1942), Gwendolyn Brooks (*A Street in Bronzeville*, 1945), Owen Dodson (*Powerful Long Ladder*, 1946), and the poets who will be remembered for their experimentation with verse during the 1950s and 1960s are part of the procession that followed the golden days of the Harlem Renaissance.

When that period ended and all writers were scattered, Negroes fought back once more to educate themselves. All-black colleges such as Spelman, Hampton Institute, Atlanta University, Clark, and Virginia Union were formed and the United Negro College Fund began.

MEET THE AUTHORS

James Baldwin was born August 2, 1924, in New York City, the oldest of nine children living in a Harlem ghetto. As a teenager, Baldwin preached after school in a small church. One can see the influence of the King James Bible on his writing and he tells of those experiences both in *Go Tell It on the Mountain*—his first book, a semiautobiographical novel—and his play *The Amen Corner*.

A multitalented man, Baldwin was a novelist, essayist, and playwright. His works have been collected into books and have been highly praised as writing of the highest quality. His novels and plays have often received mixed reviews, perhaps because they often dealt with the Civil Rights question in a way not acceptable to most Americans.

Baldwin spent most of his literary apprenticeship in the bohemian atmosphere of Greenwich Village, but in 1948 he followed in the footsteps of many other black artists and writers and lived in Paris for eight years.

Giovanni's Room (1956) dealt solely with the white world and Paris. In 1955, his collection of essays *Notes of a Native Son* established his worth as an essayist.

When Baldwin returned to the United States in 1957, he became an active participant in the Civil Rights struggle and stated his beliefs in his next book of essays, *Nobody Knows My Name*.

On November 17, 1962, *The New Yorker* magazine awarded Baldwin almost all its editorial space for a long article on the Black Muslim separatist movement and other notes on the Civil Rights struggle. The article was published in book form in 1963 as *The Fire Next Time*. His play *Blues for Mister Charlie* appeared on Broadway in 1964 to mixed reviews.

Perhaps Baldwin's greatest accomplishment was *Go Tell It on the Mountain*, which some scholars believe represented a link between the black writings of the 1930s and 1940s and the newer, more revolutionary writing being introduced by up-and-coming black writers.

William Wells Brown was the first American Negro novelist and the linking factor with which slave narratives and literary works were joined. Although he wrote during the same period as Douglass and Charles Remond, only Brown's writing evolved into what might be considered a literary career.

Born in Kentucky of slave parentage, he grew up a slave. His narrative of slave life in the United States, called *Clotel*, was the story of Thomas Jefferson's housekeeper. In his later writings he revealed the fact that he was also a slave, and some have branded that as abolitionist propaganda.

Brown was taken to St. Louis as a young boy and there he served an apprenticeship to antislavery editor Elijah P. Lovejoy of the St. Louis *Times*. Later he found his way to Canada and, in his own words, "commenced lecturing as an agent of the Western New York Anti-Slavery Society."

Brown wrote novels during the years 1849–1854, a period of time that he spent in England fighting for antislavery; thus some of his books were first published in London. He died in 1888.

Charles Waddell Chesnutt, born June 20, 1858, in Cleveland, Ohio, has been called a pioneer of the color line by both biographers and writers. His work was more masterful than that of his contemporary Paul Laurence Dunbar, and he had the distinct honor of having his short stories published in *The Atlantic Monthly*.

Chesnutt was a married school principal in North Carolina at the age of twenty-five, but in spite of his successful position, he moved his family to Cleveland because he was distressed by the way Southern blacks were treated. In Cleveland, he became a practicing attorney and wrote in his spare time, trying to fulfill a childhood dream of becoming an author.

Chesnutt published more than fifty works—short stories, essays, a biography of Frederick Douglass, and three novels—between the years 1855 and 1905.

In August 1887 his story "The Goophered Plantation" appeared in *The Atlantic Monthly*, the first time the magazine accepted a story by a black person.

His works were often ironic and authentic. His tales of color prejudice were so well written and subtly told that readers often missed his point. But he handled the scenes realistically and used his writing as a means of social protest.

He is considered to be one of the great black writers and his works have been favorably compared with those of de Maupassant, Turgenev, Henry James, William Faulkner, and James Baldwin.

Lydia M. Child, who was born February 11, 1802, in Medford, Massachusetts, and died October 20, 1880, in Wayland, Massachusetts, was a prominent white novelist who turned to writing on behalf of Negro equality. Her book *An Appeal in Favor of That Class of Americans Called Africans* was published in Boston in 1833.

A pioneer in children's literature and crusader for women's suffrage and sex education, Child took up the role of abolitionist with the same zeal as her other beliefs. With her husband, also an active abolitionist, she edited *The National Anti-Slavery Standard* from 1841 to 1849.

Her other works include the first children's monthly periodical in the United States, books on women and their problems, and books urging the adoption of sex education.

Frederick Douglass was born February 7, 1817, in Tuckahoe, Maryland. As an infant, he was separated from his slave mother and never knew his white father. He lived with his grandmother in Maryland until the age of eight, when his owner sent him to Baltimore to live as a house servant with the Hugh Auld family.

Mrs. Auld defied state law and taught Douglass how to read and write. When her husband declared that learning would make the boy unfit for slavery, Douglass continued his learning in secret.

Later in his life, around the age of seventeen or eighteen, he was "hired out" to be a ship caulker. He tried to escape in 1833, but was not successful until five years later. He fled to Massachusetts to elude the slave hunters.

In 1841 in Nantucket, Massachusetts, Douglass told an antislavery convention of his feelings and experiences as a slave. The experience catapulted him into a new career as an agent for the Massachusetts Anti-Slavery Society.

He wrote *My Bondage and My Freedom* in 1845 to combat skeptics who doubted that he could ever have been a slave. In 1882, the book became *The Life and Times of Frederick Douglass*.

After the book was published, Douglass left on a two-year speaking tour of Great Britain and Ireland so that his former owner could not capture him. In Europe, he experienced an atmosphere free of racism and was amazed at the freedom it gave him. While there he won new friends for the abolition movement.

Back in the United States, he started a newspaper, the *North Star*, and used it as his voice in the antislavery movement.

During the Civil War, he advised President Lincoln on the role of the black American in the war. He also enlisted blacks for military service. From 1865 to 1877, he fought for full Civil Rights for freedmen and supported the Women's Rights movement.

Douglass was also involved in business and political affairs, having been elected to the presidency of the Freedmen's Bank and Trust Company in 1874 and winning numerous political offices after 1877.

Douglass was the first black citizen to hold high rank in the U.S. government. He died in Washington, D.C., in 1895.

William Edward Burghardt DuBois was a contemporary of Chesnutt, Dunbar, and Booker T. Washington. He was born in Great Barrington, Massachusetts, on February 23, 1868, and died in Accra, Ghana, on August 27, 1963. A sociologist, he was the most important black American protest leader during the first half of the twentieth century.

DuBois graduated from Fisk University in 1888 and was the first black American to earn a Ph.D. from Harvard, in 1895. He began contributing essays to *The Atlantic Monthly* in 1897 that are still considered finely written and amazingly insightful. In 1903 his writings were collected and published in one volume, entitled *The Souls of Black Folk*.

DuBois clashed with Booker T. Washington and took the lead in founding the Niagra Movement in 1905. He was also a factor in organizing the NAACP in 1909.

In 1961 DuBois joined the Communist Party, moved to Ghana, and renounced his American citizenship. He died there in 1963. DuBois is probably best known for founding the newspaper called *The Crisis*. He remained its editor until 1933.

Paul Laurence Dunbar, born June 27, 1872, was the son of former slaves. In spite of the fact that he was the only black student in his Dayton, Ohio, high school, he was the popular editor of the high school newspaper.

Oak and Ivy was Dunbar's first privately printed work, published in 1893 while he was working as an elevator operator in Dayton. He sold copies to the passengers in order to pay for the printing. *Lyrics of a Lowly Life*, published in 1896, cemented his literary career and national reputation. His poems were in the minstrel tradition, which was enjoying large popularity at that time.

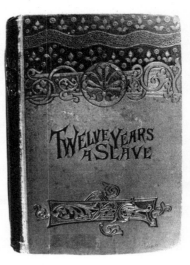

A leatherbound first edition of the autobiography of Solomon Northrup entitled *Twelve Years a Slave*. *Courtesy of Valerie Bertrand Collection; photo by Donald Vogt.*

Illustrated page from *Twelve Years a Slave* by S. Northrup. *Courtesy of Valerie Bertrand Collection; photo by Donald Vogt.*

Black Cato, a book in the Little Canary Series, by Mrs. M. A. Osgood. Lee and Shepherd Publishers, 1872, illustrated. *Courtesy of Gwendolyn Goldman; photo by Donald Vogt.*

Dunbar's prose followed his popularity as a poet. His short stories and sketches appeared in the *Saturday Evening Post* and other magazines while his novels—*Folks from Dixie, The Strength of Gideon, In Old Plantation Days,* and *The Heart of Happy Hollow*—appeared during the early years of the twentieth century.

Dunbar was not considered a good novelist but, according to one critic, would have mastered the art of fiction had he lived longer and worked more conscientiously at developing his art.

In his lifetime, Dunbar wrote seventeen books, including poetry anthologies, novels, and short story collections. He was one of the first black American writers to attempt to live off his talent and one of the first to gain national prominence. He died in Dayton on February 9, 1906, in poor health and with a good many personal problems.

Ralph Waldo Ellison's first book, *Invisible Man,* was published in 1952 and was hailed as a major contribution to American literature. Though he was a contemporary of Richard Wright, his work bore little resemblance to Wright's. His novel, a story about a Southern Negro who goes to Harlem, won the American Booksellers fiction award in 1953.

Born in Oklahoma City, Oklahoma, on March 11, 1914, Ellison was a shoeshine boy, jazz musician, and freelance photographer. He left Tuskegee Institute in 1936 and joined the Federal Writers Project in New York City.

After his collection of essays *Shadow and Act* was published in 1964, Ellison lectured on Negro culture, folklore, and creative writing and taught at various universities.

Jupiter Hammon, a slave who belonged to a Mr. Lloyd of Queens Village, Long Island, was the first Negro to publish poems in America. His first poem, "An Evening Thought, Salvation by Christ with Penitential Cries," appeared in 1760.

Most of his poetry is religious. However, one of his best-known works is a prose piece entitled "An Address to the Negroes of the State of New York City," which was made on September 24, 1786.

Frances Ellen Watkins Harper was first published in Philadelphia in 1854 when she was twenty-nine (*Poems on Miscellaneous Subjects*). She read her poems widely and was dubbed an elocutionist. Ten thousand copies of her first book were sold in the first five years. Her second book, *Moses, A Story of the Nile,* was published in 1869.

Using her fame to fight for liberation of her people, she wrote articles and letters raising questions about slavery and its effect on black Americans. In 1873 her third book, *Sketches of Southern Life,* was published, and is notable for the language its black characters used. She frequently contributed to *Godey's Lady's Book.*

George Moses Horton was a slave in North Carolina when Weston R. Gales published his volume of verse entitled *Hope of Liberty* in 1829. Horton was approximately thirty-two at the time.

He was well known among college students at Chapel Hill and was able to make a bit of a living from selling his writing. After he won his freedom in 1865, he published a second volume of verse titled *Naked Genius.*

(James Mercer) Langston Hughes was born in Joplin, Missouri, on February 1, 1902. His career as a writer began when he was a high school student in Cleveland, Ohio. His first piece appeared in 1921 in *The Crisis,* a national magazine. He was nineteen years old. The piece was entitled "The Negro Speaks of Rivers." The poem was widely reprinted and was probably the most read poem of that year.

Five years later Hughes's first book, *The Weary Blues,* was published and many volumes followed after that. He wrote "Harlemese" and his sources were "street music." He has often been called an American original.

Hughes has been considered the force that led the rest of the world to witness the black experience in the United States. His poetry captured the essence of jazz and was said to have been influenced by Carl Sandburg and Vachel Lindsay.

He attended Columbia University from 1921 to 1922 and left to live in Harlem. A few months later he boarded a freighter bound for Africa and wandered around Europe for a while. When he came back from his sojourn, he began sending out the poems he had written and, in 1925, won an *Opportunity* magazine poetry prize. In 1926 he was the winner of the Witter Bynner Undergraduate Poetry Award.

When he met Vachel Lindsay in a Washington, D.C., hotel where Hughes was a busboy, the meeting turned out a success and led to a scholarship to Lincoln University in Pennsylvania. By 1929 two of his books had been published.

During the 1930s he became preoccupied with political militancy and his poetry reflected his feelings. He traveled throughout the Soviet Union, Haiti, and Japan and served as a newspaper correspondent in the Spanish Civil War. During that decade, he also published collections of short stories and in 1940 his autobiography, *The Big Sea,* was published.

When he died in New York City on May 22, 1967, Langston Hughes had twenty-seven books in print and Arthur Springarn called Hughes the most translated contemporary American poet.

Joseph H. Ingraham was a black writer whose works are consulted today mostly by historians. His novels, published by newspapers during the late 1830s and 1840s, were extremely popular. As a young man, Ingraham toured southwestern Mississippi and wrote his first book, *The South-West,* about what he observed there. It was published anonymously in 1835.

James Weldon Johnson's first work of prose was published in 1912 and was entitled *The Autobiography of an Ex-Coloured Man.* It was not well received. By the time it was republished (and renowned) fifteen years later, Johnson was serving the National Association for the Advancement of Colored People (NAACP). The book's reissuance was partly due to the Harlem Renaissance.

A good many other events followed in the book's wake. Johnson wrote black folk sermons, which were published in a volume called *God's Trombones,* and doors were opened in the United States that had previously been closed to black Americans in the arts. (For more about Johnson, see Chapter 11, "Music.")

Illustration from the book *Slavery and the Slave Trade. Courtesy of Valerie Bertrand Collection; photo by Donald Vogt.*

William Johnson's Diary of a Free Negro was a record that he kept for sixteen years and passed on through his family. In 1938 the family entrusted the diary to two historians who published it thirteen years later.

James W. C. Pennington (1809–1870) received his Doctor of Divinity Degree from Germany's University of Heidelberg in the 1840s.

When a young man in Washington County, Maryland, he was trained as a stonemason and blacksmith. He fled slavery around 1830 and was aided by a Pennsylvania Quaker who sent him to Long Island, New York, where he acquired enough education to teach in Negro schools. He studied theology in New Haven, Connecticut, and spent some time as pastor of the African Congregationalist Church there.

While attending various European conferences, Pennington was invited to speak before aristocrats in London, Paris, and Brussels. His autobiography, *The Fugitive Blacksmith*, was published in 1849 and his book *The Origin and History of the Colored People*, the first major history of black people, was published in 1841.

Pennington was a prominent antislavery leader who fought against discrimination on public conveyances, worked on programs outlining theology, and denounced affronts to first-class citizenship.

Lucy Terry was the slave of Ensign Ebenezer Wells of Deerfield, Massachusetts. She was probably the first American slave to write poetry. Her poem described the bloody Indian raid on Deerfield in 1746. Although she was not versed in syntax, she provided a vivid picture of the massacre of the settlers by Indians on August 25. She married a free Negro and enjoyed a reputation as a storyteller, never knowing the impact she would make on history.

Gustavus Vassa wrote a rare autobiographical account of eighteenth-century slavery entitled *The Interesting Narrative of the Life of Gustavus Vassa, The African.*

Named Gus Vassa by a Swedish captain on one of his many sea voyages, he traveled extensively, eventually exploring the Arctic. He was one of few slaves to become educated, and used his education to write a journal that told of his and other slaves' trials and sorrows.

Phyllis Wheatley was the slave of Mr. and Mrs. John Wheatley of Boston. She was brought from Senegal, Africa, in 1761 when Mrs. Wheatley wanted a companion. Mrs. Wheatley purchased a sickly looking girl and taught her to read and write.

Phyllis amazed Boston with her poetic talents. She published a volume of poetry in 1773 as well as dedicating some of her poems to a Mr. Thornton, Lady Huntington, Lord Dartmouth, and others.

When her health failed, Boston doctors suggested she take an ocean voyage. Wheatley went to England, where she published her *Poems on Various Subjects: Religious and Moral* in 1773. While there she was presented to King George III. For a time after that book was published, she was the best-known American poet. Her poems were commended by George Washington and other prominent figures of her time.

Phyllis Wheatley married a black grocer named Peters, but the marriage proved unsuccessful due to the differences in their talents and temperaments.

Wheatley died in 1784, an accomplished American poet.

George Washington Williams, a serious historian of the Negro race, published a two-volume *History of the Negro Race in America from 1619 to 1880* after researching the subject from 1876 to 1883. The work was received with excitement in scholarly circles, and is regarded as the best book on Negro history written during the nineteenth century. Williams also wrote a *History of Negro Troops in the War of the Rebellion*.

Carter Woodson, editor of the *Journal of Negro History* from 1916 to 1946, made that publication one of the most influential of its time. He has been called the "Father of Black History."

Richard Wright (1908–1960) wrote about the violence and opposition he experienced during his lifetime.

Wright was born into a poor family in Natchez, Mississippi.

Down South by Rudolf Eickemeyer and Joel Chandler Harris, copyright 1900, shows pictures throughout the South. *Courtesy of Valerie Bertrand Collection; photo by Donald Vogt.*

His father deserted his mother and her two children after the family moved to Memphis, causing his mother to place Richard and his brother in an orphanage until she could save enough money to get them to their grandmother in Jackson, Mississippi.

While Wright was in high school, his mother suffered a stroke which left her bedridden for ten years. Wright left Jackson after high school and headed for Memphis. Determined to be a writer, he took jobs merely to survive, borrowed books from the library, and read himself to sleep every night. It was during this constant study of the written word that he realized words could be used as weapons.

He saved for two years in order to take his brother and invalid mother to Chicago. Wright had left one kind of prejudice behind only to deal with the Depression, which left Negroes struggling to survive in whatever way they could.

In 1935, he became a member of the Federal Writers Project, moving to the project's New York chapter in 1937.

In 1938, Wright won a $500 prize for his book *Uncle Tom's Children*. The following year he received a Guggenheim fellowship as well as the Spingarn Medal from the NAACP. The book launched Wright to fame. His readers realized that he handled his themes with authority and an intelligence that demanded he be heard out.

Native Son, his second book, was considered even better than his first and appeared as a Book-of-the-Month Club selection. In the next fifteen years, nearly fifty translations and foreign editions of his books ensured his fame worldwide.

His third book, an autobiography entitled *Black Boy*, was published in 1945 and gave evidence that Wright's range was expanding. It is currently used nationwide as part of the college curriculum for human services and psychology courses as well as in the study of American literature.

After that book, Wright moved to Paris and became one of Europe's most celebrated American expatriates. *The Outsider* (1953) was published after an eight-year silence but was not quite up to the quality of his earlier works. In the remaining years of his life, the books which were published did not meet the quality of his first works. It is said that once Wright went to Europe and no longer had to fight against prejudice, the anger that induced his brilliant writing cooled and so did his talent.

Poems of Cabin and Field, by Paul Laurence Dunbar, leather-bound. *Courtesy of Valerie Bertrand Collection; photo by Donald Vogt.*

PRICE GUIDE—BOOKS BY AND ABOUT BLACK PEOPLE

AUTHOR/BOOK TITLE   APPROXIMATE VALUE

Andrews, E. A., *Slavery and the Domestic Slave Trade in the United States,* 1836, Boston .... $25–$45

Aughey, J. H., *The Iron Furnace: or Slavery and Secession,* 1863, Philadelphia .... $10–$18

Barbour, Floyd P., *The Black Power Revolt,* 1958, New York ....$8–$10

Benet, Stephen Vincent, *John Brown's Body,* 1954, New York .... $5–$8

Blake, W. O., *The History of Slavery and the Slave Trade Ancient and Modern,* 1860, Columbus .... $15–$20

Bledsoe, Albert T., *An Essay on Liberty and Slavery,* 1856, Philadelphia........................ $45–$60

Boston Massacre—*Trial of William Wemms, James Hartegan, etc., Soldiers of his Majesty's 29th Regiment of foot, for the murder of Crispus Attucks, Samuel Grey, etc.,* 1770, Boston .... $1,200–$1,500

Bowlan, Grace Duffie, and Morgan, Ike, *Young Folks' Uncle Tom's Cabin,* 1901, Chicago ....$4–$15

Brown, H. Rap, *Die Nigger Die,* 1969, New York ... $4–$8

Brown, Ina Corrine, *The Story of the American Negro,* 1936, New York.......................$8–$12

Burton, Frederick R., *American Primitive Music with Special Attention to the Songs of the Ojibways,* 1909, New York .... $10–$15

Cable, George W., *The Negro Question,* 1888, New York .... $40–$50

Caldwell, Erskine, *Tobacco Road,* 1940, New York .... $25–$45

Campbell, George, *White and Black: The Outcome of a Visit to the United States,* 1879, New York .... $32–$45

Carey, H. C., *The Slave Trade, Domestic and Foreign: Why it Exists and How it May Be Extinguished,* 1859, Philadelphia.................................. $15–$25

Child, Mrs. Lydia M., *An Appeal in Favor of that Class of Americans called Africans,* 1836, New York .... $60–$85

Cobb, W. Montague, *The First Negro Medical Society: A History of the Medico-Cherchurgical Society of the District of Columbia, 1884–1939,* Washington, D.C.......................... $30–$35

Cohen, Octavius, R., *Highly Colored,* 1921, New York .... $32–$40

Colwell, S., *The South: A Letter from a Friend in the North with Reference to the Effects of Disunion upon Slavery,* 1856, Philadelphia... $60–$75

Cleaver, Eldridge, *Post Prison Writings, Speeches,* 1969, New York ....$7–$10

———, *Soul on Ice,* 1968, New York................ $20–$30

Cowley, M., ed., *Adventures of an African Slaver,* 1928, New York ....$8–$10

Curtis, James, *Black Medical Schools,* 1971 .... $5–$7

Davidson, Basil, *Black Mother: The Years of the African Slave,* 1951 .... $4–$8

Davis, Thomas T., *Speech on Equality of Rights,* Washington, D.C., 1866.......................... $28–$35

Dewees, Jacob, *The Great Future of America and Africa: An Essay Showing Our Whole Duty to the Black Man, Consistent with Our Safety and Glory,* 1854, Philadelphia................... $70–$90

Douglass, Frederick, *Life and Times of Frederick Douglass,* 1962 reprint, 640 pp. .... $3–$5

———, *My Bondage and My Freedom,* 1857, New York .... $10–$25

———, *Narrative of the Life of F. Douglass: An American Slave, Written by Himself,* 1845, Boston.. $30–$75

DuBois, W. E. B., *The Souls of Black Folk,* London, 1905 .... $25–$35

Eastman, Mrs. Harry H., *Aunt Phyllis's Cabin or Southern Life as It Is,* 1852, Philadelphia.. $60–$80

Ebony, Editors of, *The Negro Handbook,* 1967, Chicago .... $5–$7

Eldridge, Eleanor, *Slave Narrative,* 1842 .... $100–$150

Elliott, Reverend Charles, *The Bible and Slavery,* 1857 Cincinnati...................................... $5–$8

Essien-Udom, E. U., *Black Nations, A Search for an Identity in America,* 1962, University of Chicago ....$7–$10

Ferman, Louis, *Negroes and Jobs,* 1969, Michigan... $5–$8

Folsom, Montgomery M., *Scraps of Song and Southern Scenes,* 1889, Atlanta .... $15–$20

Frazier, E. Franklin, *The Negro in the United States,* 1949, New York...........................$6–$10

Furnas, J. C., *Goodbye to Uncle Tom,* 1956, New York .... $5–$8

Green, Lorenzo J., *Negro in Colonial New England,* 1942, Washington, D.C. .... $35–$45

Greenidge, C. W. W., *Slavery,* 1958, New York..... $3–$6

Halsey, Margaret, *Color Blind: A White Woman Looks At the Negro,* 1946, New York............$9–$14

Harris, Joel Chandler, *New Stories of the Old Plantation. Told by Uncle Remus,* 1905, New York ....$5–$10

———, *On the Plantation,* 1892, New York .... $25–$35

———, *Plantation Pageants,* 1889, Boston .... $65–$85

———, *The Tar Baby,* 1904, New York............. $20–$30

———, *Uncle Remus,* 1881, New York .... $100–$175

———, *Uncle Remus,* 1957, New York .... $5–$10

———, *Uncle Remus, His Songs and His Sayings,* 1881, New York .... $375–$450

5
Dolls

ON COLLECTING BLACK DOLLS

The most important criterion in collecting black dolls is to decide whether or not you *like* the doll. A cherished "baby" gains more nostalgic value if she/he becomes a treasured member of the household and is passed from generation to generation.

Condition is another important factor to consider when buying a doll. Clothes and wig should be original in order for the doll to command top price. The wig must also not be soiled or restyled, the skin of the doll should be clean and unblemished, and if the doll has "sleep eyes," they should open and close easily.

Though you hear about antique dolls constantly setting new records, one can begin a doll collection with a small budget. Modern black dolls can still be found at yard sales and flea markets for very little money. You may have to hunt around to find original clothes, but that exploring only serves to make collecting more interesting.

When one decides to collect black dolls, one must be prepared to compete with some of the most gregarious collectors in the antiques business. Doll collectors are probably better organized and more likely to go to great lengths in pursuing their "finds" than any other collectors. Doll collector clubs abound throughout the world and are often the best place to track down the doll of your choice.

Although rag dolls are the most common black dolls, one can find other nineteenth-century dolls made of different materials, and the novice doll collector is often pleasantly surprised by the availability and appeal of those dolls made between 1900 and 1940.

Interestingly, these dolls carry with them a bit of history as well. During the Civil War, medicines and drugs were sometimes smuggled to Confederate soldiers inside a doll's head, and ships carrying dolls were once accorded neutrality when traveling between nations at war. It was not unusual for a black doll to be sent through enemy lines, supposedly destined for its young mistress's arms, but instead torn apart once inside a military camp so that Confederate doctors could find the laudanum, bandages, or medicines stored within the doll's body. Because black people were considered beneath the whites, so were playthings made to resemble blacks. No one gave a second thought to a worn-out black rag doll. They would rather be rid of it than have it hanging around, reminding them of the basic reason they were fighting that bloody war.

Store-bought dolls were a true luxury for the children of the early black Americans. Slaves, as well as other Americans, made dolls for the young females of the family. If the family was to move, often the young one's cherished doll was the first thing left behind.

The earliest homemade black dolls were extremely crude and few have survived. They were made from bedposts, buckskin, or any fabric the makers could lay their hands on. The favorite seemed to be the rag doll. Usually made from pieces of leftover cloth, rag dolls were cherished possessions of both city and farm girls. The dolls were dressed in calico, muslin, or even feed bags. Regional dress was usually not evident, but corn-husk and nut-head dolls were prevalent in rural areas.

Eventually rag dolls were manufactured in quantity with their facial designs stamped on a piece of cloth and the bodies cut out, sewn together, and stuffed. Though factory-made stuffable black dolls are usually found bearing a resemblance to Aunt Jemima or "Mammy," I have seen some that appear to be likenesses of actual children. It is eerie to find a doll whose face is so realistic, but exhilarating as well because these lithographed cutouts are rare and considered a find.

Rubber dolls were first manufactured in 1855 by Benjamin Lee of New York; celluloid dolls were produced a decade later by John Wesley and Isaiah Hyatt. During the 1870s a Kentucky firm made dolls' heads from a new mixture that became known as "composition." Black dolls were made in all three materials, but are more common after the 1920s.

Although European manufacturers are responsible for most of the dolls made from early times through the beginning of the 1800s, American manufacturers produced the first commercial black rag dolls, as well as stuffed and plastic black dolls.

(Facing)
A rag doll whose clothing tells us she was made in the first part of the twentieth century. Her face is embroidered, dress and petticoat all handmade, shoes painted black, and she has real human hair. *Courtesy of Kristin Duval, Irreverent Relics; photo by Donald Vogt.*

Three small (under 7″) Civil War–era rag dolls with original clothes. The one in the middle looks quite angry! *Courtesy of Rose Fontanella; photo by Donald Vogt.*

An uncut "Darkey Doll," patented August 15, 1893. *Courtesy of Rose Fontanella; photo by Donald Vogt.*

FOLLOWING BLACK DOLLS THROUGH TIME

Dolls made in slave quarters on plantations are more often rag dolls, yet there have been a number of wonderfully carved wooden dolls that have survived the ravages of time. One would imagine that a working slave would not have enough spare time to construct more than two or three dolls in a lifetime; thus we cannot point to one specific person as "doll maker."

Before the Civil War, dolls were made to resemble Mammies. Often we find them holding tiny white babies, which would symbolize the Mammy's role in the household. Perhaps Mammy herself made the doll, or her husband may have made it as a Christmas gift for the child. One wonders why Mammies more often than not are ample-bosomed. One also wonders who mothered the Mammy's children since she was so often responsible for all the white children of the plantation, leaving her little time for her own.

Two prime examples of lithographed rag dolls. The smaller one appears to have been a photograph, possibly of a child who died. *Courtesy of Rose Fontanella; photo by Donald Vogt.*

After the Civil War, black dolls began to take on richer trappings, to look more like the middle class into which they would slowly move. But the transition was not a fast one and one still finds many rag dolls wearing poor clothing until well into the twentieth century.

As time rolled on, character dolls found their way into the kitchen, as objects that held whisk brooms or were made into doorstops and toaster covers. No matter what their use, plaything or utilitarian, these dolls are seen more as objects of folk art than as the playthings they were originally intended to be.

Black dolls have been mass-produced along with white dolls since the beginning of the twentieth century. Before World War I, American doll makers, as opposed to European ones, tended to play up the comic aspects of the dolls they made.

During the 1920s, 1930s, and 1940s, black dolls were cheaply made and often were just painted versions of white dolls. Not until the 1960s were black dolls made to represent black people. Celebrities such as Diahann Carroll's character "Julia" began to appear on the toy shelves of department stores.

Composition babies were sold during the early 1940s by major department stores. Some were jointed, some had painted faces, some even had little tufts of hair sticking out of their heads to which tiny bows were attached. All were relatively inexpensive and, for the most part, modeled after white dolls.

On the other hand, topsy-turvy dolls, which originated as early as the Civil War, made the best of both worlds. The doll, usually dressed in a long dress that covered her bottom half, would be black on one side and, when turned over, would reveal a white face. Topsy-turvy dolls continued to be made throughout the years and can be found in rubber, plastic, celluloid, and composition.

Hard plastic dolls were made during the period from the late 1940s to late 1950s. The black dolls made during this era were the identical mold of a white doll, finished in a brown color.

Vinyl dolls have been made from 1950 and are still being manufactured. The dolls are attractive, but sometimes the vinyl does not allow for the finer details that the early bisque and composition forms did. However, the vinyl dolls are more representative of the black race and give a truer rendition of black persons.

Cloth black dolls have been made by hand for well over 150 years. However, one must recognize that cloth dolls have been manufactured in the United States and other countries as well, and sometimes it is hard to tell the original hand-sewn example from the one that was mass-produced. If you know how to tell hand-stitching from machine-stitching, you have one step toward recognizing the difference. The next step is to check the doll's features. If they are hand-stitched as well as the clothing and the limbs, chances are you have an original. If some parts of the doll are machine-stitched, you must take a long, hard look at the rest of the doll to determine whether or not it was homemade.

Cloth dolls take many shapes and were used for a number of purposes. Toaster covers, dinner bells, pincushions, brooms, dusters, doorstops—all have been made in the form of black dolls. Examples of some are included in this chapter, and I have also included some examples in Chapter 10, "Kitchen Collectibles."

KINDS OF COLLECTIBLE BLACK DOLLS

APPLE AND NUT DOLLS

These dolls are truly American dolls, their origins firmly anchored in American soil. Little girls would anxiously await the day Mama was to bake one of her mouth-watering pecan pies because they would surely get the leftover nuts to make dolls.

Once the nut was chosen for the head, other materials were used to complete the rest of the doll's body. Wood, twigs, cloth—whatever could be used for arms and legs—were utilized. Once the doll itself was made, the work of making suitable clothes began. Again, whatever material was available was used.

Nut dolls became extremely popular in the South and were often made in pairs, one male and one female. Blacks were portrayed as they were in life. Mammies, cotton pickers, farm workers, and maids are some of the characters made from nuts.

EFFANBEE DOLLS

The Effanbee Doll Corporation, makers of successful commercially made dolls, was formed in 1913 by Bernard E. Fleischaker and Hugo Baum.

Effanbee dolls are usually marked on the back of the head and/or on the upper back.

Among the black dolls made by Effanbee are the beautiful black Grandes Dames made in 1981. The four dolls are dressed in authentic-looking turn-of-the-century costumes, complete with wide-brimmed hats and veils. There are also Negro versions of Baby Face, Half Pint, Baseball Player, Football Player, Prize Fighter, Basketball Player, Sailor, Fair Baby, Sweetie Pie, Twinkie, Butter Ball, and Sugar Plum.

In Effanbee's 1970 catalogue, almost every doll had a "Negro version." By 1971 the dolls were still being made as copies of the white dolls, but now the catalogue description called them "black dolls." From 1970 on, black dolls were included in every collection, but still as copies of the original white dolls. In 1980 the catalogue shows a Miss Black America doll as discontinued under its International Collection line.

Effanbee produced a limited edition set of 125 black versions of four of the Grandes Dames for a mail-order collectors' doll company called Treasure Trove in 1981.

Black Currier and Ives Skaters were issued as a special set in 1980 and Black Miss U.S.A. was the 1982 special.

Because of the many discontinued versions of Effanbee dolls through the years, it is suggested that you check your doll against a book that details Effanbee dolls and the years in which they were in production in order to date your doll more accurately.

JOEL ELLIS DOLLS

Joel Ellis of Springfield, Vermont, made a doll out of green maple wood during the mid-nineteenth century. He patented this type of doll, but did not make many because of heavy competition from imported bisque dolls.

The penny wooden Joel Ellis dolls were highly mobile because of their distinctive wooden joints. He often painted the doll's metal boots black, but sometimes the hands, also metal, were painted white.

Ellis dolls also all have curved fingers. The sizes of dolls are basically 12″, 15″, and 18″. The Negro Joel Ellis dolls had painted faces and are difficult to find because the dolls were manufactured only during 1873.

FAIRCHILDREN NEW ENGLAND RAG DOLLS

The FairChildren dolls are made by Helen Pringle of Aledo, Texas, and will surely be the Joel Ellis and Izannah Walker dolls of the next century.

Pringle handmakes all the dolls of stuffed cotton cloth. Their arms, legs, and heads are painted with oil paints and they are usually 32″–36″ tall, although a smaller version can now be ordered. They are seam-jointed at the shoulder, hip, and knee and have applied ears.

Pringle hand-paints the dolls' faces to resemble naive or primitive eighteenth- and nineteenth-century children's portraits and the clothing is usually antique or replicas of antique clothing.

Pringle makes both male and female dolls, each having its own name, and no two are ever alike.

In her own words, Pringle reports: "When a doll is commissioned, the buyer may select the hair, eye, skin, and costume colors, as well as general era and look of the doll, for example 'country child' or 'city child,' dressed for church or as a ragamuffin, or any special request that I am able to execute."

Each doll is stamped with a maker's mark, signed, and numbered on the body. The price of a doll, at the time of publication, is between $400 and $500. All FairChildren New England Rag Dolls are protected by design and name copyright and are not to be copied or duplicated in any way.

FOLK ART DOLLS

The title "folk art dolls" is a very general description and needs to be clarified a little.

Many folk art dolls, Civil War era and pre–Civil War, were made out of whatever material the maker had on hand. Straw was used for stuffing, and faces and clothes were made with leftover bits of fabric and thread, perhaps even a glamorous piece of material left over from the master's lady's dress. The dolls were made to be playthings, not to be sold. They were made by hand and the majority of them weren't signed. If you do find a signed doll, however, the price of your acquisition will certainly be higher than its unsigned sister's.

Izannah Walker, one of the early manufacturers who made folk art–type dolls, came from Rhode Island and did her work around 1870. Her black dolls, made with wool hair, are extremely rare and highly prized.

Other handmade dolls, of the clay variety, were made by Rosa Wildes Blackman of Homer, Louisiana. Blackman was a white woman who made dolls during the 1940s and is well known for her "true Southern Negro types." Some of her dolls are part of the collection at the Brooklyn Children's Museum.

Creating beautiful black infant dolls during the turn of the century was Leo Moss's goal in life. Today his creations sell for thousands of dollars. Each one is recognizable by the tear on its puzzled face.

Apples, dried to be wrinkled like an old woman's face, were often used as faces for folk art dolls. Walnuts, pecans, and chestnuts became parts of dolls as well.

Black bottle dolls, the body and dress fitted over a bottle filled with sand or rocks to weight it, were often made by the homemaker and used as doorstops. Most of these dolls were made in the "Aunt Jemima" tradition—complete with apron, kerchief around the head, and hand-sewn features.

Corn husks, clothespins, spools, papier-mâché—all were made to resemble dolls. Whatever the maker had available for materials was used.

Wear should be expected when one shops for folk art dolls. These dolls weren't put away in a box to be saved for future generations. They were kissed, hugged, taken to bed, spanked, bathed, dressed, undressed, and dressed again. They were loved and they tend to pull our heartstrings a little more if they show the wear and tear of a small child's adoration.

SOME MAKERS AND TYPES OF BLACK DOLLS

Cameo Doll Products/Strombecker Doll Corporation made a 19″ black baby in 1973 that they called "Miss Peep." The baby resembles early bisque babies, but is all vinyl with inset brown eyes. It is marked "Cameo" on the back of its head.

Deluxe Topper Toys made a series of 6″–6½″ teenage dolls. Of these "Dale," a black woman wearing a minidress; "Van," a black football player; "Dancing Dale"; and "Dancing Van" were black. The dolls all had snapping knees and a jointed waist. The Dale dolls had rooted black hair and painted eyes while the Van dolls had molded hair. The dolls were made in the early 1970s.

Fisher Price Toys made a black cloth-and-vinyl doll in 1973 that they called "Elizabeth." The doll was 14″ tall, had rooted black hair, painted brown eyes, and was marked "18/168630/ 1973 Fisher Price Toys" on the back of its head.

Hasbro Toys has made black versions of quite a few of their dolls. One of the best known is "G.I. Joe." In 1965, Hasbro put out a 12″ black G.I. Joe Soldier complete in combat fatigues. "Soul," a black woman with an Afro, dressed in wildly colored bell bottoms and accessories, was distributed in 1971, while 10″ "Leggy Sue," dressed in a turtleneck evening gown, was one of a set of four distributed in 1972.

Horsman Dolls were started by E. I. Horsman in 1865. They began producing bisque dolls shortly after they opened.

Horsman's synthetic rubber and early vinyl process has always been considered among the best in the doll field. They have made and distributed black versions of their dolls for the past thirty years.

Ideal Toy Corporation has been in business from 1902 and continues to operate. They marked their early dolls with their name enclosed in a diamond and later used just the imprinted name. Often dolls were marked with the words "Made in U.S.A." and identifying numbers.

Ideal was the first company to manufacture dolls with sleep eyes, in 1915. It was also the first company to use plastic. In 1933, this futuristic firm developed "magic skin."

Ideal's baby "Thumbelina" was made in both black and white versions as were the "Velvet" dolls. "Baby Belly Button," made in 1970, was all vinyl with rooted black hair and painted brown eyes.

Madame Alexander was originally from Russia, but her four daughters started a doll business in New York City, the Alexander Doll Company, in 1924. Beatrice ("Madame Alexander") supervised the making of the dolls. All dolls were tagged with the name "Madame Alexander" on their body or on clothing tags.

Madame Alexander dolls have always been noted for their beautiful costumes. Many dolls are made for a period of a year, then offered for several years more before being discontinued. Because of that, Madame Alexander dolls are highly desirable and rise quickly in value.

Some of Madame Alexander's black dolls include "Cynthia," 15″, made in 1952; "Baby Ellen," 14″, made in 1965; and "African," 8″, marked on back "African by Madame Alexander," made in 1966.

Maggie was a doll artist who made a pair of black dolls she called "Nicodemus" and "Nicodemus Girl" in 1966. The dolls were all stained ceramic/bisque with fur wigs and were marked "Maggi Head/1966" on their heads.

Mattel, Inc. is best known as the company that made the Barbie doll, but they have made other dolls as well and continue to be a major toy-producing firm.

The company was started in 1945. The "Barbie" doll was introduced in 1958 and Barbie's black friend, "Francie," was introduced in 1967. In 1968, "Christie" was introduced. "Julia," from the television show of the same name that starred Diahann Carroll, was brought out in 1970, and that same year "Brad," a dark-skinned male with an Afro, was put on the market.

Other black dolls manufactured by Mattel include a black "Chatty Cathy" (1962), black "Baby Say n See" (1967), black "Talking Drowsy" (1968), black "Swingy" (1969), black "Bouncing Baby" (1969), black "Baby Go Bye Bye" (1970), black "Valerie" (1971), black "Betty Beans" (1973), and black "Peachy" and her "Puppets" (1973).

Novelty Dolls have been made out of all kinds of materials including corncobs, pipes, dried fruits, rubber nipples, nuts, clothespins, and other strange materials. Often these dolls were made as souvenirs of certain areas of the country.

Penny Woodens were made in the early eighteenth to twentieth centuries. These dolls were thus named because they were made of wood and sold to New Englanders in the mid-nineteenth century for a penny.

Most penny woodens are under 4″ tall, although there are taller ones with more elaborate hairdos. Their hair is painted black with a center part, their bodies are jointed at the shoulders, elbow, hips, and knees, and the head shape varies with each doll.

Black penny woodens are rare, but they can be found.

Rag Dolls. At the same time that wooden folk toys were popular in New England and Pennsylvania with the children of families who could afford to have their offsprings' portraits painted alongside their favorite toy, the children of slave families in the South were nurturing the only toy they may have had through their entire childhood—a handmade rag doll.

Hobbyhorses, jointed wooden dolls, and dollhouses were toys for the well-to-do, the families that could afford to pay the folk carvers who traveled from house to house peddling their wares and their talents.

The dolls a black girl may have had in her life were more than likely made by her mother or an aunt, probably consisting of scraps of leftover material, and more than likely stuffed with hay or cornstalks. If she was lucky, it might have had a piece of lace or some pretty buttons donated by members of the "big house"—the plantation owner and his mistress.

The dolls can be simple or sophisticated, unrealistically homely or uncommonly beautiful. But all have appeal. And most have been loved just as much, perhaps more, than their fancier sisters.

Remco Industries had the rights to make Kewpie dolls for only two years, 1968 and 1969. During that short period, they made a 7″ black Kewpie of plastic and vinyl. It was marked "7AJLK/2/Cameo" on the head, "Kewpie" on its foot, and "Cameo" on its back. Remco also made an 18″ doll they called "Gingersnap." Gingersnap was marked "Doll:E4/Remco Ind. Inc./1968" on the back of its head.

Sears sold a black doll from 1910 to 1940 called "Chubby Kid." This Kewpie-like doll was 8″ tall, made of composition, with painted features, a watermelon mouth, jointed arms, and a black mohair wig. The reference book in which I checked did not give the maker of this doll.

Sun Rubber made a 17″ black baby doll that they dubbed "Colored Sun-Dee" in 1956. She was made of vinyl with brown sleep eyes and came with her own nurser. She was marked "Sun-Dee/Sun Rubber 1956" on her head.

Topsy-Turvy Dolls were often black on one side and white on the other. Sometimes they were made in the form of nursery characters, such as Little Red Riding Hood on one end and the Grandmother on the other, or the plain and fancy Cinderellas. They originated out of the same needs as a rag doll—as a toy for the little girls of the family at a time when the family utilized every scrap of material and energy. The unique point of the topsy-turvy was that it gave the little girl two dolls to play with instead of one.

A broom doll wears her hat jauntily and carries her nut babies like groceries. She has wonderful details, original clothes and basket; we date her 1870–1885. *Courtesy of Rose Fontanella; photo by Donald Vogt.*

A long-legged "bedroom" doll, a usually homemade type popular during the 1920s and 1930s. *Courtesy of Jan Thalberg; photo by Donald Vogt.*

Topsies were made before the Civil War as well as during and after and are still being made today.

Uneeda Doll Company made a few black dolls, including "Littlest So Soft" and "Teenie Toodles." Both dolls were made of plastic and vinyl.

Vogue Doll Company began after World War I. Jennie Graves, the original owner of the company, began by making doll clothes and importing German dolls. Vogue has undergone quite a bit of growth since then, but its "Ginny" doll is still highly collectible. Vogue has made black Ginny dolls as well as black baby dolls. They continue to be in business today.

Izannah Walker worked in Central Falls, Rhode Island, and was described by her niece as "deploring the fact that she was not a man." She was quite a busy person, dabbling in more than one business at a time when a working woman was frowned upon.

Walker used a hand press to mold the bodies and heads of her dolls out of glue-stiffened fabric which was reinforced with webbing and stuffing. She made the dolls at home, working for many years to improve her craft. In 1873, she obtained a patent for her special design.

Walker did make some black dolls, but they are difficult to find and rather expensive.

(Above)
A "nutty" family includes everyone from the preacher to the babies; all are 2″ or under. *Courtesy of Rose Fontanella; photo by Donald Vogt.*

(Left)
A trio of bottle dolls, all of different vintage and materials, but all totally original. *Courtesy of Rose Fontanella; photo by Donald Vogt.*

Male rag doll. His finely sculpted head and facial features are all fabric, he has all his genitals, his fingernails are quills, and his shoes are a sewn part of his body. *Courtesy of collection of Gene and Linda Kangas; photo by Gene Kangas.*

Three composition babies—the one on the right an Effanbee—all in good shape. *Courtesy of Rose Fontanella; photo by Donald Vogt.*

Boy and girl stocking dolls, 7" and 6" tall, respectively. His face is painted, hers is embroidered and her clothes are made from scraps. *Courtesy of Kristin Duval, Irreverent Relics; photo by Donald Vogt.*

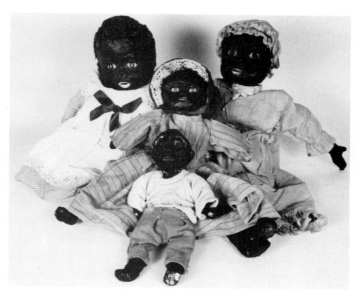

Papier-mâché dolls, all made around the turn of the century and all in original dress. *Courtesy of Rose Fontanella; photo by Donald Vogt.*

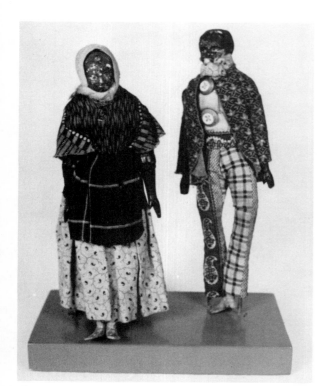

An early papier-mâché slave couple. On their stands the dolls achieve a lofty height of 7". *Courtesy of Rose Fontanella; photo by Donald Vogt.*

A gentlemanly rag doll dressed in a checkered hat, paisley jacket, red-and-white striped pants, and paisley shoes. His facial features and hair are all hand-sewn. *Anonymous private collection, courtesy of Ken and Ida Manko; photo by Donald Vogt.*

Two rag dolls made during the Civil War or immediately before. Their dresses are original and condition is fairly good. *Courtesy of Rose Fontanella; photo by Donald Vogt.*

An elongated black gentleman dressed in velvet jacket, red double-breasted vest, white pleated shirt, black checked pants, and bow tie. His face is velvet, the nose is prominent, and his teeth and eyes are hand-sewn. *Anonymous private collection, courtesy Ken and Ida Manko; photo by Donald Vogt.*

The woman in the Victorian hat is definitely the matriarch of this doll family. All are hand-sewn and date to the late 1800s. *Courtesy of Rose Fontanella; photo by Donald Vogt.*

A group of topsy-turvy dolls. One end of the doll has a black face (above) while the other end has a white face (below). *Courtesy of Rose Fontanella; photo by Donald Vogt.*

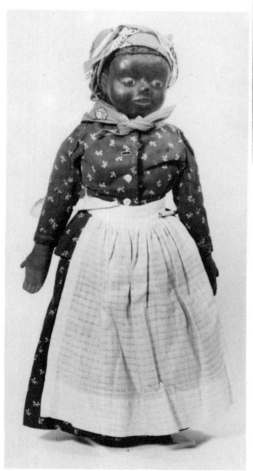

Black doll, ca. 1870. The face and shoulders are molded and painted, the body and limbs are cloth, and the hair appears to be human. *Photo courtesy of Collection of Barbara Kramer.*

PRICE GUIDE—DOLLS

DESCRIPTION OF DOLL APPROXIMATE PRICE

Amos 'n Andy, jointed wooden doll, 5½" .... $350–$400

Aunt Jemima, child, Diana and Wade, oilcloth, boxed...$90–$105

Automaton, Dancing Dolls, one black male, one black female, 1880s, 10" .... $350–$385

Baby Crissy, boxed.. $75–$95

Baby Yawnie, boxed, 14"............................... $20–$30

Bisque, glass eyes, lace outfit, 11".................... $32–$45

Bisque, jointed arms and legs.......................... $10–$15

Bisque, jointed, girl, three ponytails, 6"............. $10–$15

Bisque, Miss Topsy .... $15–$20

Bisque, Musical Action, head and hands bisque, plays music.. $15–$25

Bottle doll, black, gray dress, checked apron, bandana, earrings, 13"............................... $32–$40

Bottle doll, early ....$95–$110

Bottle (milk) doll, Black Mammy, original clothes, ca. 1910.................................... $35–$50

Bye-Lo Baby, bisque, jointed arms and legs, gown, 4".. $15–$20

Celluloid black baby, pink dress, three braids ...... $45–$55

Chatty Baby, original clothes....................... $75–$95

Chatty Baby Brother, 15"............................. $65–$85

Cloth black baby, talks, glass sleep eyes, 18" .... $100–$150

Cloth doll, all original, 1880s, 14½".............. $250–$300

Cloth doll, blue dress, red bandana, 10"............ $22–$30

Cloth doll, Mammy, embroidered face, red-and-white checked dress, 15½" ....$65–$100

Cloth doll, Mammy, pearl eyes, earrings, kerchief, apron, 9".................................... $30–$50

Cloth doll, yarn hair, ca. 1940 ....$75–$100

Cloth dolls, made by Ursuline nuns in New Orleans, hats real silk, souvenirs, 3" ....$85–$100

Cloth dolls, pair, one 7" with very large whites around eyes, handmade, long white cotton dress; other large Mammy with kerchief, hand-stitched, homespun dress, appliquéd and sewn features................................. $240–$300

Composition, unmarked, jointed, molded hair, three yarn braids, 14"........................... $100–$120

Composition, unmarked, jointed, molded painted hair, painted eyes and mouth, some damage .. $45–$50

Composition baby doll, with pigtails, some damage... $40–$50

Composition doll, Man Friday, handmade, fur shirt, 8½".. $75–$95

Composition topsy-turvy doll, jointed shoulders, 7"... $65–$80

Cream of Wheat man, cloth.......................... $45–$65

EEGEE Toys dolls, girl, blue suede dress, shoes and ankle socks, black rooted hair, sleep eyes.. $15–$20

Effanbee, Black Butterball.............................. $25–$35

Effanbee, Fluffy, Negro, official Girl Scout uniform... $15–$20

Effanbee, Little Tubber, black, boxed, 10" .... $15–$20

Effanbee, Lucifer, puppet, ca. 1937................$85–$100

Effanbee, Negro girl, painted eyes, molded hair, ball-jointed, composition body, dressed, 14"... $150–$175

Frozen Charlotte, 1"................................... $30–$40

Gerber Baby, boxed..................................... $35–$45

Happy Baby, giggles and coos, 16".................. $18–$22

Horsman Dolls, Baby Bumps, 12"................. $200–$250

Ideal, Black Baby, 1971, 14"........................ $20–$25

Ideal, Grow Hair Crissy............................... $35–$40

Ideal, Tiny Tears, dressed in panties only, 13" ..... $10–$15

Madame Alexander, African, 8".................... $275–$325

Madame Alexander, Black Baby, Ellen, 14" ..... $100–$125

Madame Alexander, Black Cynthia, 18" .... $575–$625

Madame Alexander, girl, French, 8"............... $40–$60

Madame Alexander, Leslie, ballerina .... $250–$300

Mammy, handmade, patterned dress, painted face, 1930s.. $48–$55

Mattel, Hush Little Baby .... $14–$18

Mattel, Julia, 1968, in box........................... $35–$40

Norah Wellings, black child, glass eyes, hoop earrings, 13½"................................ $165–$180

Nut doll, Mammy, 8".................................. $15–$20

Oilcloth doll, Uncle Mose........................... $35–$45

Paper dolls, Uncle Mose and Aunt Jemima, uncut... $78–$90

Papier-mâché, black child, jointed, hair, c. 1885, 6½" .... $200–$250

Papier-mâché, Mammy .... $225–$245

Papier-mâché, shoulders and head, mohair wig, inset pupilless glass eyes, 9½".................. $200–$250

Rag doll, Aunt Jemima, approximately 16"......... $40–$60

Rag doll, black boy, button eyes, embroidered features, ca. 1930.................................... $28–$35

Rag doll, black dress and jacket, embroidered face, human hair .... $125–$160

Rag doll, black girl and boy, c. 1890, all original, 11"... $250–$275

Rag doll, blue kerchief, matching skirt, button eyes...$85–$100

Rag doll, Cream of Wheat, black man, printed on fabric, 17"............................... $55–$95

Rag doll, girl, black stocking body, embroidered face, gray dress, white apron, pantaloons, black karakul-type hair, 20".................... $110–$150

Rag doll, knitted fabric face, embroidered features, dressed, 23"............................. $150–$180

Rag doll, Little Sister, detailed features.............. $25–$35

Rag doll, Mammy, many layers of clothes........ $110–$140

Rag doll, Mammy, stuffed and hand-stitched, dressed in red and white .... $30–$40

Rock-a-Bye Baby, cloth body, sleep eyes, 7½" .. $245–$270

Saucy Walker, 22" .... $90–$110
Souvenir doll, marked "New Orleans, La." .... $8–$10
Terri Lee Co., Brown "Jerri," plastic, 20" .... $200–$225
Topsy-turvy, black and white .... $110–$130
Topsy-turvy, black and white, inked faces, 10½"... $35–$75
Topsy-turvy, bottle doll .... $165–$180
Toddler, painted side eyes, original fur hair,
    12½" .... $125–$140
Ventriloquist's dummy, clothed .... $1,800–$2,000
Vinyl, boy, Shindana Toys, 1972 .... $35–$50
Vinyl, stuffed, Aunt Jemima, Uncle Mo and
    two kids .... $150–$200

Vogue, Black Baby Dear, signed .... $20–$30
Vogue, Ginny .... $15–$20
Wax, mohair wig, painted eyes, cloth body,
    14" .... $225–$300
Windup, Louis Armstrong .... $80–$100
Wooden, black man with top hat, Wm.
    Hennessey, 1868, 12½" .... $450–$500
Wooden, Mammy and Pappy, nineteenth
    century, dressed as poor people, 9" .... $250–$300
Wooden, Walking Mammy, 1940s .... $15–$20
Wooden, walnut, man carrying bag of cotton,
    12" .... $35–$50

EVERY SATURDAY

AN ILLUSTRATED WEEKLY JOURNAL.

Vol. II. Whole No. 60.]　　　SATURDAY, FEBRUARY 18, 1871.　　　[Price, 10 Cen

6

Ephemera

Ephemera is anything that has temporary interest or value. Into this category fall most paper goods, such as newspapers, magazines, posters, playbills, postcards, and trade cards.

To obtain a clearer view of the field, one must explore the fields of publishing and advertising, as well as become familiar with the personalities (or subject matter) one is interested in collecting. For example: should you decide to collect ephemera about black Americans during the Civil War period, you could learn about the newspapers and magazines of that day, the politicians in power, the household trends, the military, and so on.

Ephemera is one field that infringes on all the other areas of collecting. There are clubs, antique shows, and shops devoted to this field. For those in your area, consult your local antiques/collecting trade papers.

HOW TO COLLECT EPHEMERA

Because paper does not withstand the test of time, it is most advisable to keep your collection in acid-free mats or, if possible, period frames. Trade card and postcard collectors can file their collections in albums made especially for that purpose. These albums can be found in most large stationery or department stores.

Remember that if you glue your collection into a scrapbook, you are losing the value of those objects you diligently hunted down. Should you choose to sell all or part of your collection, you would have a hard time doing so if they were glued.

Condition of paper goods is important, but don't pass up a newspaper or other article with information or photos of black Americans because the piece is a little dog-eared. The older the newspaper (or paper article), the more likely it is to be brittle or damaged. A collector must take into consideration the very definition of ephemera when collecting: "anything that has temporary interest or value."

To help you understand what you are collecting, there follows a brief historical outline of black politics. By knowing a little about what happened to black Americans at different points in America's history, you can better decide on which era you are going to concentrate.

Transatlantic trade of Negroes by Puritan merchants brought wealth to early New Englanders. Boston and Newport prospered from the trading of slaves, which can be traced back as far as 1638. Because New England did not have a plantation economy, the Negro population was kept relatively small—fewer than 17,000 slaves were based in New England out of a total of 660,000 throughout the rest of the Colonies.

In the seventeenth century, 887,500 slaves were imported. An all-time high of 7 million was reached in the eighteenth century.

Quakers such as George Fox, William Penn, John Woolman, and Anthony Benezet wrote, printed, and distributed antislavery literature. Benezet even took blacks into his Philadelphia school where he taught them how to read and write.

The Civil Rights Act gave slaves citizenship in 1866, and in June of the same year blacks got the right to vote. Black men started entering politics and began making a decisive difference in the way an election would turn. During the late 1800s, disgruntled white former slave owners organized to form the Ku Klux Klan and other anti-Negro organizations and unleashed their fury on the black population.

The Niagrara Movement, formed by W. E. B. DuBois in 1905, became the National Association for the Advancement of Colored People (NAACP) in 1910.

Franklin Delano Roosevelt's presidential years saw some of the most important changes in black history since Abraham Lincoln's presidency. The National Youth Administration, Civilian Conservation Corps, Work Projects Administration, and Federal Writers' Project each, in their own way, worked to help the unemployed black people. Eleanor Roosevelt kept her husband in touch with black women's issues and even invited the Council of Negro Women to the White House, a gesture that was not looked upon with favor by most of her husband's constituency. More than that, Mrs. Roosevelt withdrew her membership in the Daughters of the American Revolution when that club refused to let black soprano Marian Anderson sing in Constitution Hall. Mrs. Roosevelt arranged for the concert to take place outside the Lincoln Memorial.

The most "action" in black history, besides the Civil War era, took place in the 1950s and 1960s when the Civil Rights movement was in full swing with people like Martin Luther King, Jr., at the forefront (see biography below). And history

(Facing)
Every Saturday cover, Saturday, February 18, 1871, "Getting Breakfast for the Old Man," illustrated by W. L. Shepard. *Courtesy of Gwendolyn Goldman; photo by Donald Vogt.*

continues to be made, giving us an endless number of subjects to collect.

TYPES OF EPHEMERA

ADVERTISING

See Chapter 1 for further information on advertising.

MAGAZINES

By the end of the eighteenth century, some 100 magazines had appeared in the United States. Each offered entertainment and/or uplifting information for the average white American citizen. Magazine publishing did not have a solid base in the United States until after the Civil War.

During the mid-nineteenth century, illustrated magazines became more common. *Leslie's Weekly* and *Harper's Weekly* were the forerunners in this new phase of the magazine industry. During the Civil War, *Leslie's* had as many as twelve correspondents at the front and was able to give a good pictorial record of the war. *Leslie's* and *Harper's* are sources for stories (fiction as well as nonfiction) about blacks during this time. Though few of the actual magazines found are perfect and intact, one can often find etched covers and frontispieces that have been matted and framed, among them well-done views of blacks during the Civil War and Reconstruction. The magazines often ran articles about slavery and different points of view on the subject. Humorous stories and scenes of black life were also subjects of interest in these early magazines.

Once the British repealed the advertising tax in 1853, advertising in magazines became more common. *Harper's* did not want advertisers to invade its pages until the 1880s, and some magazines did not allow advertisers until the mid-twentieth century. This fact made a difference in the amount of revenue the magazines procured, but it also allowed them to maintain higher standards without bowing to the wishes of advertisers who were designing ads derogatory to black Americans.

Now a fine line is trod between a magazine and its advertisers. The publication of the wrong kind of article can lose thousands of advertising dollars. Since magazines now are supported by black advertisers as well as white, one can see how the financial success of black America can filter down to the buying public in many different ways. When American blacks did not own businesses—because they were not allowed to—they did not advertise, and therefore had no say in what the American public learned about them. Thus myths started and were perpetuated. Once blacks entered the business world, learned the ropes, and began to enter their own ads in national publications, they could slowly begin to chip away at the buildup of years and years of subliminal prejudicial suggestions. Advertising continues to have a very strong impact on the magazine publishing industry.

News and photo magazines, such as *Time* and *Life*, began to appear in the early twentieth century. Their job was to summarize the news, expand it, make it more concise or more attractive. In other words, they supplemented newspapers, but did their job in a glossier, more varied format. Now black reporters and journalists entered the magazine field on a regular basis (see the biographies of Bruce Davidson and Danny Lyon in Chapter 12). Black people were becoming the photographers instead of the subjects.

The picture magazines were spurred on by the development of new, miniature cameras. *Life* began in November 1936 and was publishing a million copies within a couple of weeks. "Digest" magazines started with *Reader's Digest* in 1922 and soon expanded to include others such as the *Negro Digest* and *Jet* (1951). Black political and scholarly journals were formed to appeal to the segments of society interested in these subjects, and were often published by the same firms that published mass-market magazines.

The twentieth century brought about the decline of magazine publishing's most expansive phase. All magazines, including those aimed toward black Americans, now tend to be moving away from general interest and toward specialization.

NEWSPAPERS

People have needed to know what is going on around them for centuries and for this reason, newspapers—in one form or another—have been a part of society since the first Roman gazette was published daily in 59 B.C.

The first Negro newspaper, *Freedom's Journal*, was published by Samuel Cornish and John B. Russwumn in New York City on March 16, 1827. It was followed twenty years later by Frederick Douglass's newspaper, *The North Star*. Douglass, a famous abolitionist, dedicated himself to pleading the American Negro's case before a mostly uncaring public (see his biography, Chapter 4).

After the Civil War, Negro journalism grew rapidly and several periodicals joined the ranks of the "political press." By the turn of the century, Negro America was experiencing a surge of upward mobility and that sign was clear in the number of new publications entering the field.

W. M. Trotter, editor of the Boston *Guardian*, was one of the most noted Negro editors. He often found himself at odds with Booker T. Washington and was considered quite a radical. The Chicago *Defender*'s editor, Robert Abbott, was known for his efforts in mass circulation and his distinctly different use of headlines.

Although the Negro press was concerned with keeping the black public informed of black views, it also reported their feelings on issues of the day. The periodicals became a powerful political tool and were often the targets of violent acts as responses to radical editorials or unpopular remarks by outspoken editors.

Eventually Negro businessmen formed self-support groups such as the NAACP and the National Negro Business League to better their lot, but in the early days the Negro reporter found his life not to be an easy one.

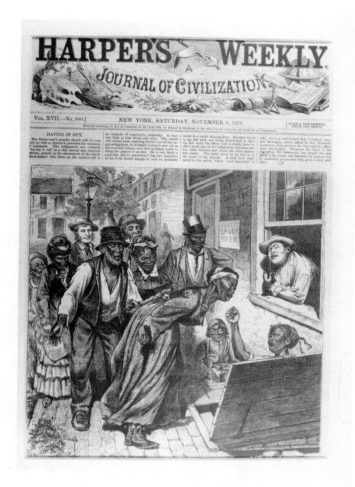

(Above)
Harper's Weekly cover, Saturday, November 8, 1873, "Having It Out." *Courtesy of Gwendolyn Goldman; photo by Donald Vogt.*

(Top Left)
March 25, 1893, *Judge* cover, political satire, "Uncle Sam's Cabin." *Courtesy of Gwendolyn Goldman; photo by Donald Vogt.*

(Left)
Thomas Nast engraving, "President Lincoln Entering Richmond," dated February 24, 1866. *Courtesy of Gwendolyn Goldman; photo by Donald Vogt.*

Photograph of Booker T. Washington, Tuskegee, Alabama, August 12, 1901. *From the collection of Mildred Franklin.*

During the post–Civil War era, one of the most prominent black journalists was T. Thomas Fortune. Fortune attended Howard University but never finished, having left his studies to marry. He learned the newspaper business at a number of Eastern newspapers before editing *The Globe*, a Negro daily. Along with Booker T. Washington, he formed the National Negro Business League in 1900.

The black press supported black self-help groups, but also kept the black public informed on vital community issues, such as education and police protection.

During the world wars, black journalists and their periodicals backed the United States during its time of need. Yet as soon as there was a peaceful hiatus, the press turned their interests toward becoming volatile leaders in the pursuit of civil rights. Roy Wilkins, a journalist in the Midwest in the 1920s and 1930s, was recognized by the NAACP for his work to further the cause.

Some newspapers were so adamant in their beliefs that the Justice Department threatened them with sedition charges in 1942 and it became increasingly difficult for those papers to find newsprint.

The black papers suffered the same ailments most American newspapers did after World War II. With the increasing popularity of radio and television, newspapers were taking a back seat. White papers, stronger metropolitan dailies, and national magazines began to hire top black journalists to cover the black community. The smaller black papers did not have enough power to hold their employees, nor could they offer them the salary of the larger papers.

During the late 1960s and early 1970s, black newspapers began to rally and the National Newspapers Publishers Association, which represented over thirty black papers, began to schedule workshops that served to put black journalism back on a more positive level. Today there are almost 150 black journals and two of the dailies, the *Atlanta World* and the Chicago *Daily Defender*, have circulations of over 30,000.

POSTCARDS

Postal cards could not be mailed in the United States until 1873. It is thought that the first picture postcard was not mailed until 1893.

Following the Civil War period postcards of black military, farmers, or workers were made with regularity, and they are considered desirable in today's market. The black subjects of the early hand-tinted postcards were depicted in their normal habitat as well as in typically black American scenes. As with all early black American ephemera, the gist of the postcard was usually downgrading the Negro. Those postcards that just show a black work group, cowboys, or minstrels are often more valuable to a collector because they depict the "professional" black of that era instead of the black as the white person chose to see him.

The heyday of the picture postcard was from 1900 to World War II. The use of postcards as tourist mementos widened their appeal, and many have ended up unused and unposted in

Photo postcard, "Mischief Brewing." *Courtesy of Malinda Saunders; photo by Donald Vogt.*

"Once Upon a Time," photo postcard of old man telling story to two boys. *Courtesy of Malinda Saunders; photo by Donald Vogt.*

postcard albums and collections. This was also the era when black comic postcards were in style. Cards that showed a large black woman, her back to us, saying, "I'se a lil' behind in mah writin'," were the norm instead of the exception. The linenlike photograph postcards that began to be circulated in the 1920s showed such scenes as a mother picking lice out of her children's hair or an old man driving a mule touted as the "only transportation in Atlanta." It was also during this period that cards depicting black cotton workers and blacks eating watermelon were common. Some postcard collectors have told me that they only collect those cards.

Postcards derogatory to blacks were being sent up to the time of the 1960s Civil Rights movement.

POSTERS AND PLAYBILLS

Printed or written announcements that were publicly displayed have been found dating back to the wall paintings of Egypt and Assyria. The earliest printed paper posters began to be made in Germany during the latter half of the fifteenth century and in England around 1476.

Posters circulated before and immediately following the Civil War having a connection with black America are usually slave auction posters or "wanted" posters. These early posters were often letterpressed and not of a large size like our posters today. Because newspapers were bought only by those citizens who could afford them—and who could read—posters were a way of spreading news of an upcoming event. Slave auctions were advertised this way during the early days of our United States, but it is rarely that we find one of these early posters intact.

More commonly found are later posters demanding the recovery of runaway slaves or Civil War soldiers. Plantation owners often advertised large rewards for the return of their "property," which may have encouraged the bounty hunter to keep the poster as proof that the offer had been made and to ensure that payment for return of the slave was made also.

Artists were inspired to lend their talents to designing posters that resulted in the beautifully illustrated works of the Victorian era. Advertising posters from this era that feature blacks are among the most striking and colorful that a collector will find.

The work continued to improve and posters during World War I are the most attractive of any American wartime posters. Artists such as Will Bradley, Maxfield Parrish, Charles Dana Gibson, and Howard Chandler Christy are among some of the American illustrators responsible for the marvelous artwork depicting black fighting men on posters dating from 1880 to 1920.

Posters after World War II are often just large photographs, but strong artistic portrayals of the Civil Rights movement and the Black Power movement are the most graphic in their political statements. One such poster was printed in 1967 and illustrated by children's book illustrator Tomi Ungerer. The top border reads "black power," the bottom border "white power," and the illustration shows a black person holding and eating a white person's foot while the flip side shows the white person doing the same. It is a very effective depiction of the strongest black/white feelings since the Civil War. But this time, the feelings were positive.

TRADE CARDS

Trade cards began to appear as early as the late seventeenth century and carried advertisements for businesses of all kinds. They reached their peak of excellence in the nineteenth century when they were often embellished with vignettes illustrating the trade the card advertised. The cards were beautifully inscribed using copperplate engraving. (See Chapter 1 for more information on this kind of advertising.)

PROFILES OF BLACK AMERICAN NEWSMAKERS

Abda, a mulatto slave who belonged to one Thomas Richards of Hartford, Connecticut, was the bastard son of a Negro woman and a white man. He ran away in 1702 and lived with a Captain Wadsworth, also of Hartford.

Richards sued Wadsworth for the return of his property, and was answered by Abda's countersuit for damages. Abda claimed that, because of his white blood, his enslavement was illegal. Abda was declared free by the Inferior Court of Common Pleas held in Hartford in 1704.

Other slaves, including Adam, the slave of Judge Saffen of Boston, and Caesar, who belonged to Richard Greenleaf of Newburyport, followed Abda's example and won their cases.

Some Negroes, such as Cambridge Moore, Caesar Prescott, Caesar Jones, and Caesar of Griswold, Connecticut, earned their freedom by serving in the colonial or revolutionary armies. Also freed during the Revolution were Negroes who composed parts of Tory estates, or runaway slaves such as Crispus Attucks.

Sadie T. M. Alexander was the first black woman admitted to the Pennsylvania Bar, in 1927. She also served as chairperson of the Philadelphia Commission on Human Relations, was the secretary of the New York Urban League, and was also appointed by President Harry S. Truman to the U.S. Commission on Civil Rights.

Mary McLeod Bethune (1875–1955) was the founder and president of Bethune-Cookman College. She also served as adviser to President Franklin D. Roosevelt, was president of the National Council of Negro Women, and is considered by most to be the most influential woman in black American history.

Joseph Burnett II, known as "Bus Bus," was a free Negro landowner and the first free Negro slaveholder in New England. He lived during the late 1700s.

Shirley Chisholm is a lawyer and the first black person to be a candidate for the presidency of the United States. She sought the 1972 Democratic nomination. Chisholm was also the first black woman elected to Congress (1968).

THAT REMINDS ME--

I'M JUST A LITTLE BEHIND IN MY WRITING

Comic postcard, "That Reminds Me—I'm just a little behind in my writing." *Courtesy of Malinda Saunders; photo by Donald Vogt.*

Paul Cuffee was a free Negro of mixed parentage who in the first quarter of the nineteenth century became famous as a merchant, philanthropist, and colonizer. Cuffee was also a staunch Quaker who helped in the building of a new meeting house for the Friends, and was the first Negro to attempt the resettlement of freedmen in Africa.

In 1815, he helped found the Friendly Society of Sierra Leone and, at his own expense, took thirty-eight freedmen to Liberia. When Cuffee died, he left an estate estimated to be somewhere around $120,000.

Prince Hall was born in 1748 of a white English father and a mulatto mother in Barbados. He came to Boston in 1765. While he sought the means to improve the status of Negroes, he worked for the emancipation of Massachusetts slaves.

Hall began the Negro Masonry of the United States in 1787 with African Lodge No. 459. (He had been denied admission into the white Masons' lodge.) He later became a Methodist minister.

Jesse Jackson. Through the 1960s and 1970s, black history added many firsts to its lists. Probably the most significant event to end this era is the beginning of another. The Reverend Jesse Jackson emerged as a man who would move nations and come close enough to the American presidency for citizens to sit up and take notice.

Jesse Jackson has not yet finished his history-making career, but he has already helped pave the way for blacks and made the future even brighter—as did another extremely eloquent personality who comes next in this alphabetical list.

Martin Luther King, Jr., was a believer in the Gandhi way of causing change through nonviolent civil disobedience. His type of consciousness-raising came at a time when America's blacks needed a leader to show them direction and to pull them together.

With his eyes on progress and his heart full of hope, King worked through the churches of the South, right into the heart and soul of the black people. His theories worked. The black people pulled together in support of King's ideals in marches, boycotts, and sit-ins, and quiet but firm actions got the results they wanted.

People such as Rosa Parks, the woman who refused to give her bus seat to a white passenger, caused changes in the governmental structure. Because of her actions, the U.S. Supreme Court outlawed Alabama's bus segregation laws on December 20, 1956.

In early 1960, King made his first connections with then Senator John F. Kennedy. It was the first time in history that the Negro vote helped a president into office. JFK received 75 percent of the black vote and went on to fight for the Civil Rights bill. The bill was not passed until after Kennedy's assassination.

Martin Luther King, Jr., was assassinated in 1968.

Philip Randolph organized The Brotherhood of Sleeping Car Porters after fighting the Pullman Company for twelve years. Randolph's planned march on Washington to fight discrimination in war industries resulted in FDR's appointment of a Fair Employment Practices Committee to see that his executive order to stop discrimination would be enforced.

Dr. John Rock, a Boston doctor and lawyer, was, in 1858, the first Negro admitted to practice before the U.S. Supreme Court and was also the first person to say, "Black is beautiful."

Mary Church Turrell (1863–1954) was the co-founder and first president of the National Association of Colored Women. She represented black American women at three international conferences and was active in Civil Rights as well as in the desegregation of Washington, D.C.

Harriet Rose Tubman (1823–1913), famous as the "conductor" of the Underground Railroad, also served as a nurse and spy for the Union troops in the Civil War. Tubman organized the Underground Railroad, freed herself and her family, then traveled south nineteen more times to free other slaves.

Nat Turner was born a slave in 1800 and was executed on November 11, 1831. He was a preacher and considered to be the instigator of the "Southhampton Insurrection."

Turner believed he had a vision and that Negroes were to rise up and slay their oppressors. With seven friends, he murdered his master and five members of the family while they lay sleeping in their beds. The next day, Turner's group had grown to forty-five and had massacred thirteen men, eighteen women, and twenty-four children. His actions resulted in stricter slavery codes.

William Styron, author of *The Confessions of Nat Turner* (1968), used a document that Turner dictated while waiting for his execution to write the unusual novel.

Booker T. Washington (1856–1915) was born a slave in Hale's Ford, Virginia. His determination to get an education led him to walk several hundred miles to Hampton Institute to enroll in 1872. He graduated from Hampton three years later and taught in Malden, West Virginia. He entered Wayland Seminary in Washington, D.C., and later returned to Hampton to teach Indian boys.

In 1881, he was appointed principal of a small school with thirty students called Tuskegee Institute. While there, he brought the institute to worldwide attention and was invited to be the spokesman for Negroes at the Atlanta Exposition in 1895. Presidents Theodore Roosevelt and William Howard Taft sought his views and advice on the Negro in America during their times as rulers of the country.

Washington organized the National Negro Business League in 1900 and also participated in organizing the General Education Board and the Phelps Stokes Fund. He advised his people to work out their problems by helping themselves improve. He felt that this would slowly lead to an improvement of the masses and would eventually erase prejudice.

PRICE GUIDE—EPHEMERA

DESCRIPTION   *APPROXIMATE PRICE*

Article on Uncle Tom, *Harper's Weekly,*
December 21, 1861 .... $10–$15
Autographed letter to General Butler about
wages to Negroes from
Abraham Lincoln, 1862 .... $6,000–$7,000
Autographed letter to the governor of Virginia
about free Negroes from
General Robert E. Lee .... $1,300–$1,500
Autographed manuscript, *Death of Slavery* by
William Cullen Bryant, 1866..................... $25–$35
Birthday card, comical, boy taking bath, 1920s .... $1–$3
Cardboard doll, Mammy, walking.................... $20–$25
Cartoon, Currier and Ives, Darktown Cartoons,
Mule Train on the Upgrade, Downgrade
(pair).. $300–$375
Cartoon, "Poor Li'l Mose," New York *Herald,*
1901 .... $35–$45
Cover, *Every Saturday,* February 18, 1871,
"Getting Breakfast for the Old Man," illustrated by
W. L. Sheppard .... $15–$20

Drawing by Thomas Nast, subject: Emancipation,
Harper's Weekly, January 1863 .... $50–$75
Engraving by Thomas Nast, President Lincoln
entering Richmond, February 24, 1866 .... $75–$90
Greeting card, "A . . . A . . . Ah me! Goin'
away"... $5–$7
Letter opener, black boy and alligator, celluloid ... $25–$35
Lithograph, black military recruitment, U.S.
soldiers at camp, 1863.......................... $450–$550
Magazine cover, *Life,* August 1949, article on
Jackie Robinson .... $5–$7
Magazine cover, *Life,* 1965, Willie Mays............ $12–$15
Map, Amos 'n Andy, Weber City..................... $25–$35
Newspaper, "Frank Leslie's True Blue Democrat
Club," November 18, 1876 .... $15–$18
Newspaper, *Harper's Weekly,* "Bound and Free,"
New York, December 27, 1873 .... $25–$40
Newspaper, *Harper's Weekly,* New York,
November 8, 1873 .... $25–$35
Newspaper, *Judge,* political satire, "Uncle Sam's
Cabin," March 25, 1893.......................... $15–$20
Newspaper, *Leslie's,* "Courtship to Marriage,"
December 22, 1900 .... $15–$20
Paper tablet, Amos 'n Andy, picture on cover ..... $10–$15
Photograph, Amos 'n Andy, autographed,
black-and-white, with mailing envelope......... $16–$20
Postcard, A Good Crop in Dixieland,
black boy getting hair cut............................ $2–$4
Postcard, "Ah tries to be puhlite an' nice . . ." ......$8–$10
Postcard, Aspects of Slave Days, set of ten ....$6–$10
Postcard, At the Old Cabin Door, Richmond, Va.... $2–$4
Postcard, Aunt Venus hunting in Dixie Land .... $4–$6
Postcard, black boy riding turkey .... $3–$5
Postcard, Compliments of the Fifth Dimension .... $5–$7
Postcard, Comrades, two boys with arms about
each other.. $12–$15
Postcard, Cotton Ginning Day, road with carts of
cotton ....$8–$10
Postcard, cotton picking in the South, 1950s .... $4–$6
Postcard, Elks Fraternal, black baby riding goat.... $12–$15
Postcard, "Eve stole first and Adam . . .,"
comic... $12–$15
Postcard, "Goliath was struck out by David . . .,"
comic.. $6–$8
Postcard, Grand Pop embarrassed, 1940s .... $2–$4
Postcard, group of people picking cotton................ $4–$6
Postcard, "Honey, next to myself, I love you,"
comic, illustrated by Twelvetrees.................... $4–$6
Postcard, "Honey, we'se waitin' fo' you all in
beautiful Florida," two black babies sitting on
pelican's back..$8–$10
Postcard, "I'se ah comin', sugah lamp," comic ..... $12–$15
Postcard, "I'se waitin' fo' you here down south"......$8–$10
Postcard, "I wasn't born to labor," boy leaning
against cotton bale..................................... $5–$8
Postcard, Just a note, comic ....$8–$10

Postcard, "Lawsy me! What a peculiar little boy," comic .... $6–$8
Postcard, man pitching hay off wagon, photo .... $8–$10
Postcard, Mischief brewin', four black children .... $5–$8
Postcard, My Old Log Cabin, old black man chopping wood .... $5–$8
Postcard, Negro melodies, Tuck .... $15–$20
Postcard, Olde time method of cooking as used at Boscobel Farm up to 1905, photo .... $5–$7
Postcard, "Once upon a time," photo .... $10–$15
Postcard, One Jack and two black, two children and a mule .... $8–$10
Postcard, "Out on Bale," boy sitting on top of bale of cotton .... $15–$20
Postcard, picking cotton .... $1–$3
Postcard, picking cotton in Arizona, photo .... $4–$6
Postcard, "The prodigal son made a home run . . .," comic .... $12–$15
Postcard, Rapid transit at West River, Maryland ...... $4–$6
Postcard, Rapid transit in Middlesex County, Va., photo .... $6–$8
Postcard, "Rebecca went to the well . . .," comic .... $12–$15
Postcard, Rocky Mountain, N.C., Tar River baptizing .... $12–$15
Postcard, "Seben come Leben," boys tossing dice .... $8–$10
Postcard, Seven up, Children standing in row outside cabin door .... $6–$8
Postcard, Sleighing in Old Virginia .... $12–$15
Postcard, Southern products, black baby sitting in basket of cotton, photo .... $5–$8
Postcard, Souvenir of the Sunny South, "Romeo and Juliet in the Cotton Field," fold-out .... $35–$45
Postcard, Sunday morning in Dixieland .... $12–$15
Postcard, Thanksgiving Greetings, woman plucking turkey .... $10–$15
Postcard, "That reminds me . . . I'm just a little behind in my writing," comic .... $8–$10

Postcard, "That strain again," black man with homemade violin, singing .... $5–$8
Postcard, The Three Bares, 1940s .... $2–$5
Postcard, three black children eating chicken, photo .... $10–$15
Postcard, Three of a Kind, three boys sitting on fence .... $8–$10
Postcard, Two Loving Hearts .... $8–$10
Postcard, Uncle Tom, signed Detroit Publishing Co. .... $6–$8
Postcard, Waitin' fo' Mah Sweetheart .... $18–$20
Postcard, "Wanted: someone to play wif mah. Chickun preferred" .... $8–$10
Postcard, Weighing cotton, photo .... $5–$8
Postcard, "Well! Who'd A'thunk it?" .... $15–$20
Postcard, "Who said watermelon?" .... $5–$8
Postcard, woman sitting in front of fire, photo .... $3–$6
Poster, Amos 'n Andy, 1930s, 20″ × 13″ .... $75–$90
Poster, antislavery, The Negro Woman's Lamentation, 1775 .... $225–$275
Poster, Black Military Recruitment, 1862, on linen .... $1,000–$1,250
Poster, Darktown after Dark, "A Bunch of Niggerism" .... $30–$50
Poster, J. C. Rockwell's Sunny South Theatre, five different versions, each .... $95–$125
Poster, Remus on Broadway, cake walk, two step .. $30–$45
Poster, Uncle Tom's Cabin, published by Erie Litho, Erie, Pa., two sheets: Topsy's Recreation and life-sized black figure .... $440–$600
Trade card, American Negroes, black wedding day .... $8–$10
Trade card, Foster Higgins and Co. of New England, black man shaking pillowcase out window .... $4–$6
Trade card, Grown with Williams, Clark and Co.'s high-grade bone fertilizers, black woman's head on top of cotton plant .... $6–$8
Valentine, From Many Lands, black girl, Tuck .... $6–$8

Catherine Anne Bowen by Joshua Johnson, oil on canvas, ca. 1830. Part of "Sharing Traditions: Five Black Artists in 19th Century America." *Courtesy of National Museum of American Art; transfer from National Museum of African Art, gift of Norman Robbins.*

Cigar store figure, painted zinc minstrel, 10½″ tall. Made in the late nineteenth century, it is marked "Wm. Demuth & Co. Manufacturers, New York." *Courtesy of the Shelburne Museum, Shelburne, Vermont.*

7

Folk Art

Although black folk artists make up more than half of the known folk art community, they are not as well known or as fully recognized as they should be. Some have been shown and interviewed by national newspapers and/or magazines, yet their names are not recognizable to those who are not deeply involved in the folk art field.

The art of the Afro-Americans, like their music, is undeniably their own. Yet black folk arts and crafts have not been given the same attention as black music even though arts and crafts are just as important a part of American culture, if not more so.

Folk art is the expression of the common people and usually has nothing to do with the fashionable art of the times. The folk artist follows his/her own emotions and applies them directly to his/her craft. The difference between the folk artist and the fine artist is only a refinement of knowledge. The folk artist is rarely schooled, uses the tools and supplies available, and creates naive forms of art that have only recently, in the long history of antiques, become appreciated as true "works of art."

American folk art differs from European folk art in that European folk art was rooted in distinct racial or class traditions. Their patterns of design appear to be old, inherited ones created by skilled craftspeople who specialized in that art. It is difficult to tell the age of a piece of European folk art because patterns were copied and the art remained timeless; an example is the painting one sees on the sides of goat carts or horse-drawn wagons in the Mediterranean area.

Black American folk art is largely the work of men, women, and children who had little or no artistic training and no regard for what was in fashion or "acceptable" at the time. They did not copy the work of their ancestors, although there was undoubtedly some influence. They worked from the heart and designed items that were useful or fanciful, but always for them, for their use and enjoyment. They did not follow trends or traditions, just their own beliefs.

Some of the work now considered folk art was done by artisans who were professionals but were concerned with the purpose of their products rather than their beauty. Shop signs, ships' figureheads, house decorations, items considered useful, such as canes and pottery—all were made to suit a purpose.

Other types of black folk art were made by people working only to please themselves or others. This category encompasses embroidered pieces, quilts, young women's samplers, and decorative painting that artisans applied to furniture or to the walls of their masters' homes.

A good number of folk painters and craftspeople never developed their natural ability to a point where their work was recognizable, because it wasn't acceptable for blacks to have a trade or to become good at it. Most were satisfied with a small amount of public or familial attention.

The folk artists who were good enough to be considered portraitists often did other work as well; few nineteenth-century communities could support a full-time resident portrait painter. Often those other jobs included sign painting and lettering, coach and carriage painting, clock face decoration, or architectural renderings.

Itinerant folk artists, called "travelers" by their compatriots, went from town to town offering their services. They would stay in an area or in someone's home, painting portraits until their work was done. The family whose portraits were being painted would give them room and board in exchange for the paintings. One of the better-known black portraitists was Joshua Johnson. His biography will come later in this chapter.

Often traveling painters would barter their services for something they needed: food, shelter, or something as laughable as "three months' worth of shaves."

During the mid-1800s, it became the fashion for ladies of the family to be schooled in art at a seminary. This fashion made it even more difficult for the black traveling painter to find work.

Although African influence was strong during the years prior to the Civil War, after the Emancipation some of those ties were broken and we can see the black American folk artist emerging with his/her own values, styles, and forms, distinctive and truly unique.

American folk art, like the people who inhabit its lands, is diversified and reflects a broad range of expressions, talents, and emotions. It has a straightforward simplicity and displays only a basic understanding of design and color. It also shows a disarming naiveté indicative of what we know of the primitive arts. Whatever the painter felt, whatever societal influences were the greatest during his/her growth years, and whatever traditions he/she had been exposed to, were all part of what came out on the canvas, wood carving, or sculpture. Thus, each piece is unique, each is a special piece of art in its own right and in its own category. We would be hard pressed to put a price on something that we could not compare to a like object.

The work of black folk artists is distinctive in that their portrayal of Afro-Americans is more realistic than that of their Caucasian counterparts. The features of the figures done by Afro-Americans are less pronounced, the expressions on the faces are more realistic, sometimes even painful. Gone are the flared nostrils, bulging eyes, and exaggerated lips so often seen on figures painted or sculpted by nonblack folk artists.

Seen also are the deep-rooted Africanism and the belief in witchcraft and religion. The dignity with which the characterized figures hold their heads, the subdued emotional looks on their faces, the lack of grotesque overtones, makes the folk art done by blacks an extremely valuable part of black Americana, highly prized by today's collectors.

Beginning with the days of slavery, many influences contributed to the art forms that we now put under the classification of "black folk art." Carpentry, carving, pottery, grave decoration, quilting, basket weaving, and ironwork are all areas where black artisans learned their trade. From these beginnings artists created a new field.

CARVING AND POTTERY

The world of antiques knew very little about this field until a survey, done in 1937 and now part of the Index of American Design of the National Gallery of Art, uncovered an enormous amount of slave artifacts. One of those pieces was attributed to a slave carver. It is a large figure of a man, which is thought to have been at one time attached to a post. The figure was carved from one solid piece of walnut and originally painted gray-green.

A slave of the pirate Jean Lafitte was thought to have carved a pair of chickens between 1810 and 1815.

A seated preacher with an open book in his lap, now in the Art Institute of Chicago, was carved in Kentucky during the mid-1850s and because the preacher's features are extremely realistic, the work is attributed to a black American. Though only 29″ high, the piece exudes a quiet dignity, a thoughtfulness and pride, that can be felt even when just looking at a photograph of the object.

Walking sticks, carved by hand and often decorated with animals or reptiles, are now classified as folk art. One of the earliest examples of this craft is said to have been carved by Henry Gudgell, a slave blacksmith who lived in Livingston County, Missouri, during the 1860s.

Canes were thought to have been a leftover craft taught by African tribes. Indeed, if one compares an African cane to an Afro-American one, the similarities are amazing. Both commonly depict a reptile winding its way up the stick; the head of the stick is often in the shape of a human or animal. It was thought by many Africans that witches traveled as animals— bats, reptiles, black cats—in order to bring death and disease to their enemies, and this superstition can be seen reflected in American black folk art.

As strong as was their belief in witchcraft, the early slaves held fast to deep religious beliefs, and that theme comes through their work as well. In fact, there are times when one work will illustrate both the good and the evil that the early black American felt in everyday life.

Gravestones were embellished with animal figures and objects in order to drive away evil spirits. Even pottery that slaves made for their own private use frequently depicted skulls or grotesque faces. In nineteenth-century Georgia and the Carolinas, slaves were employed in plantation potteries, and the jugs they made in their free time were often tagged "voodoo pots," "slave jugs," or "grotesque jugs"—a name suggested by their very nature. It is not known what purpose, if any, these jugs fulfilled.

BASKETMAKING

Baskets have been woven by Africans and Afro-Americans for use at home and in the fields. Though functional, the baskets have become a folk art of sorts because the makers wove their own styles into the baskets they produced.

Materials used were usually pine needles and white oak strips. The materials present in baskets and the style of weaving can distinguish where a basket was made. For example, baskets made in Sharon, Mississippi, of laced strips of white oak are very different from those made in Charleston, South Carolina, where pine needles were coiled into basket forms.

In some areas of the United States, basketmaking could be considered a cottage industry, keeping their makers and their families in clothes or with a roof over their heads. But more commonly basketmaking was a necessity, made enjoyable by those folk artists with a talent for making their work an art.

In the 1920s and 1930s a roadside basket stand was a common sight in the South. Each area seemed to have its own particular style; what was sold at one stand could be completely different from the product of a stand seven or eight miles down the road.

The basketmaker used what materials were plentiful in the area: the tough, long, brown grass in the South Carolina low country, the sweet grass gathered north of Charleston, pine needles, palmetto fronds, and so on.

Although basket weavers could not sell their wares in Charleston in 1939 and 1940, makers still exist in rural areas today and pass their talents down to younger members of the family or to whoever wants to learn.

QUILTS

Quilts can be traced from slavery to the present, from Harriet Powers to the contemporary work of Pecolia Warner, Sara Mary Taylor, and Pearlie Posey. Each black family has a

Cane, ca. 1960, by Emory Papp, Aurora, Ohio (died 1979), 32" long. The handle is a likeness of Louis Armstrong, with carved and painted eyes and teeth; the stick is varnished wood. *Collection of Gene and Linda Kangas; photo by Gene Kangas.*

Grotesque pottery jug from the South, possibly Georgia. *Courtesy of Martin and Anne Ellman; photo by Donald Vogt.*

quilt maker somewhere in its past (or present) who brought her designs and artistic ability to light while working with her hands to produce something to keep the family warm.

For generations, country women have engaged in the social phenomenon commonly known as the "quilting bee." But it was not until recently that the Afro-American art of quilting was discovered by the antiques and crafts worlds.

Afro-American quilts have some distinctive qualities, as do their makers. Each is individual and striking, yet there are ways by which the quilts can be identified as being made by black Americans.

It has been noted by experts versed in Afro-American quilts that nothing but hand-picked cotton went into the best Southern quilts. Some early black quilts were sewn on a machine (the sewing machine was invented in 1846).

Appliqué, commonly practiced in Africa, seemed to influence Southern black quilt makers such as Harriet Powers,

and was often used in the designs of black quilters.

Strip quilts are compared to Ashantil and Ewe woven textiles from Ghana. The preference for red and yellow colors in American quilts is thought to have come from Ashantil preferences for the same colors in their woven cloth.

Quilt patterns were handed down from generation to generation, often accompanied by hand-wrought samplers. The style of the black American patterns was more informal and less complex than the quilts made by the Amish or their Southern counterparts. Most patterns were geometric and included the popular Sawtooth, Wedding Ring, Rising Sun, and Lone Star designs. The "crazy quilt" was extremely popular because the quilter often had only small scraps of material to work with and could randomly assemble these pieces into the informal design.

Most noticeable in Afro-American quilt designs are: strips that are used to form the basic quilt design; the use of large-scale designs; bright, contrasting colors; patterns that would be considered offbeat on other quilts of the time; and the look that the quilt was not "planned."

Whatever the comparisons in style, it is obvious even to the most naive quilt collector that black Americans were influenced by their African background, an influence that shows through not only in their quilting but in any other part of the "black Americana" folk art scene.

FAMOUS BLACK QUILTERS

Some of the finest black American quilts known to exist were made by a black American slave woman named Harriet Powers. Her quilts are now parts of collections belonging to the Smithsonian Institution as well as the Museum of Fine Arts in Boston.

Her Bible Quilt (ca. 1895, owned by the Smithsonian) is 68″ × 105″ and consists of fifteen squares in which she tells the story of the Bible from Adam and Eve to the Crucifixion of Jesus.

Powers's 1898 explanation of her quilt owned by Boston's Museum of Fine Arts reveals religious and astronomical symbols that have been interpreted as warnings to the sinful.

It is thought that her quilting style was a derivative of textiles made in Dahomey, Africa, where brightly colored fabrics were appliquéd on a dark background. The appliqué work in Powers's Bible quilts has also been compared to Fon appliquéd textiles.

Powers was born a slave in Georgia in 1837 and died on the outskirts of Athens, Georgia, in 1911. She exhibited her first Bible quilt in 1886 at the Cotton Fair in Athens. She refused to sell the quilt to University of Maryland scholar Gladys-Marie Fry at any price, but when she was in need of money four years later, Powers contacted Fry and sold it to her.

Through following visits and conversations with Powers, Fry discovered the meaning behind each detailed square of the quilt and also realized that Harriet Powers had given of herself, her beliefs, and her emotions to design the quilts that she believed to be the "darling offspring" of her brain.

Other quilt artists are included in a brochure published by the Study of Southern Culture, University of Mississippi. The brochure was written by Maude Southwell Wahlman of the university and by Ella King Torrey, and gives general information about black quilts and biographies of specific quilters.

HOW TO TELL A QUILT'S AGE

Condition is not necessarily evidence of a quilt's age. While one quilt may have been kept wrapped and only used for special occasions, another made at the same time could be in shreds from everyday use and repeated washings.

Pattern is also not evidence of age, for each pattern has gone through various stages of popularity. If one can find the name given by the quilt maker to her pattern, one has some clue to its date.

The method of construction is the only definite way of dating a quilt. Such techniques must be studied to be understood because different regions, as well as different nationalities, invented their own distinctive ways to assemble their quilting pieces.

An easy way to determine the age of a quilt is to hold it up to strong sunlight. If you see dark spots, they are cotton seeds. Although some people claim that this discovery would prove that the quilt was made prior to 1793, the date of the invention of the cotton gin, that is not necessarily so—especially with quilts made by black Americans. Often rural quilt makers did not have access to ginned cotton until many years later.

Cotton seeds in an interlining may be taken into consideration to date quilts, but still we do not have a *definite* date because some early Southern-made quilts are free of cotton seeds thanks to the laboring of black hands to prepare a padding free of seeds.

Age can also be determined by the type of material used in the quilt. Cotton was the cloth most commonly used beginning around 1815. Printed cotton began to be popular around 1840 and by 1870 had gone out of fashion. Keep in mind that the early colonists often had fabrics imported from the East or Europe. Those fabrics were completely used. If the maker of a dress had a few inches left over, that remnant was saved in a scrap bag to be used or combined with home-woven fabrics later in a quilt. Some types of bindings were used for specific periods and others were used indiscriminately.

Styles tell age. The earliest quilts—or bed coverings—were all white. Appliquéd quilts, first made at the end of the eighteenth century, are not usually found to be made by black Americans, but later designs such as the friendship quilt (popular in the mid-nineteenth century) and crazy quilts (popular at the turn of the nineteenth century) were often made by black Americans and their families.

Only a few quilt makers signed their work until after the 1840s, when the autograph or friendship quilts were in vogue.

HOW TO WASH, HANG, AND STORE QUILTS

Old quilts can be used in many different areas of the house. They can be gracefully laid across the back of a couch or chair in the living room. They can make the perfect tablecloth for a dining room harvest table or they can make any bed seem as if it belongs on the pages of *Country Living* magazine. Yet today the trend seems to be to hang your quilt, to enjoy its beauty, simplicity, and workmanship as one would enjoy a fine piece of art.

No matter what you do with your quilt, it is important to remember that quilts are delicate and must be treated with great care and respect. They may look almost new but their fibers have been weakened with age.

Examine your quilt carefully for worn spots, holes, or tears. You may wash it if you remember not to pull the fibers too strongly and not to use a strong detergent. A detergent such as one used to wash baby clothes is mild enough to wash a quilt. The safest way to clean a quilt is to wash it by hand, perhaps squeezing a little lemon juice into the rinse water to brighten

"The Creation of the Animals" by the famous quiltmaker Harriet Powers is made of pierced and appliquéd cotton with plain and metallic yarns. *M. and M. Karolik Collection, courtesy of Museum of Fine Arts, Boston.*

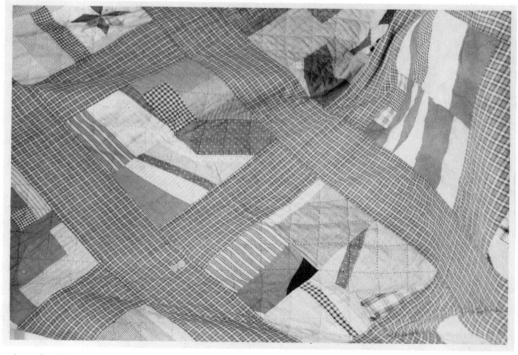

A quilt of homespun pieces, made in Georgia between 1820 and 1840. *Courtesy of Jeanie Ohle; photo by Donald Vogt.*

the colors, then place the quilt over a clothes rack or on a freshly mown lawn until it is dry. Try not to hang it on a clothesline as the wet fabric will weight down the quilt and pull on the delicate threads that hold the pieces together.

If you wish to hang your quilts, there are several ways to support the quilt and take the weight off the part you will hang. One way is to sew a binder on the edge where you wish to hang the quilt. Make it wide enough to slip a curtain rod through, and you have the perfect sleeve for hanging your quilt. Other quilt experts may tell you to make a frame for the quilt or even to put a complete backing on it before tacking the quilt (backing) to the frame and hanging it.

It is best to store your quilts in the summer as the strong sun and accompanying heat can damage them. Even humidity will affect antique quilts.

If you do desire to hang your quilt, make sure you take it down after six months and give it a rest in a closet. Line the quilt with acid-free paper and pack it loosely so that there will not be too much pressure on its fibers.

Using quilts as table covers has been frowned upon for the simple reason that they may get stained. If you decide to use a quilt as a tablecloth, take it off when having dinner and you will be able to preserve it longer. Watch the family cat as well. Cats do not know the difference between an heirloom and a good scratching post and will flex their claws without considering their owner's feelings.

SAMPLERS AND NEEDLEWORK

Embroidered pieces of linen were produced in Europe and America from the early seventeenth century on. Because sewing was a practice confined to females of the upper classes, early samplers are rare. The materials used were fragile and the passage of time has taken its toll.

The embroidered designs on the samplers of the seventeenth and eighteenth centuries were meant to teach girls a wide range of stitches as well as the letters of the alphabet and the numerals. Most samplers were dated and signed once completed and were often worked on for a long period of time. Samplers reached their height of popularity between 1830 and 1870.

Although it is difficult to determine whether the signature on a sampler belongs to a black American, there are often distinguishing earmarks. The most obvious is black figures worked into the overall design, a practice that was common in samplers made shortly after the Emancipation Proclamation of 1862. Such a sampler might announce: "We's Free."

However, if a sampler is signed but has no distinguishing black earmarks, the best way to validate it is by researching the family name. Don't be surprised if your research turns up an old white Southern family—remember that slaves often took on their master's surname.

Should you still have questions about the sampler's date, measure the piece. Early samplers were narrow; wider ones did not appear until the looms on which cloth was made got wider. The samplers made in the late eighteenth and early nineteenth century were wider than they were high. The thread is also a giveaway to the age of the piece: eighteenth-century samplers used wool thread; silk thread was used thereafter.

Do not expect to find black samplers made before 1800. Most black samplers were made in the cross-stitch pattern and the stitching is probably long, uneven, and crude.

The Connecticut Historical Society in Hartford holds a piece of needlework done by Prudence Punderson (1758–1784) entitled "The First, Second and Last Scene of Mortality." The scene shows a cradle attended by a young black girl. A woman is shown in the center of the piece and a small coffin is to the left.

TRADE SIGNS AND CIGAR STORE FIGURES

Because quite a few of our ancestors could not read, trade signs for city establishments, such as shoemakers, taverns, and cigar stores, were in the form of figures rather than letters.

Made to catch the eyes of passersby, the most common are the barber's pole, the hanging shoe that symbolized the cobbler, the upraised arm holding a hammer to mark the smithy, the watch to point the way to a jeweler or watchmaker. A tavern could be symbolized by a mug or a group of grapes, and the cigar store by a figure with a fistful of cigars or tobacco leaves.

Tobacconist's figures appeared early in the seventeenth century in England, and in America during the eighteenth century. Philadelphia wood sculptor William Rush, carver of signs and tobacconist's figures, was one of the first to make such a figure in the United States during the 1820s.

The familiar cigar store Indian was not the only personage to grace the stoop of a tobacconist's shop. In fact, the earliest tobacco-shop Indian was a strange combination—a Negro with a headdress. He was wearing a kilt of tobacco leaves and was known as the "Virginian." Obviously, the Englishman who made the figure was trying to combine all the persons known to have a connection with the tobacco crop into one figure: the slave who worked on the plantation, the "Virginian" who owned the plantation where the slave worked, and the Indian who originally introduced white settlers to the growing and smoking of tobacco.

It is a fact that the Indian was not known as a cigar-store figure until the mid-nineteenth century. The Indian enjoyed popularity outside the tobacconist's place of business from the 1850s to the 1880s.

Tobacconist's figures were usually carved by the same people who carved ship's figureheads, and often the figure standing in front of the tobacco shop seemed ready to pull away from the shore at any moment. Though the bulk of tobacconist's figures were Indians, there were also a smattering of figures made to resemble white men or women, Turks, Civil

A sampler, dated 1882, announces, "We's Free," with the help of two black dancing figures, an elephant, and a cat. *Collection of Joseph W. and Nathan Wood; photo by Donald Vogt.*

War figures, or the plantation Negro, with a wide expanse of white shirt collar. Blackamoors were also popular during the 1870s, as were minstrels and jockeys.

During the end of the nineteenth century, production of these wooden figures declined because of new ordinances that ordered the figures off the sidewalks. Therefore, toward the end of the nineteenth century, other figures appeared as "mascots" of tobacco shops. Counter-top pieces as well as figures to be placed in the shop's window were made.

Most cigar-store figures were carved out of white pine logs. First, the maker used an ax to get the general shape of the figure. From there, he would bore a hole in order to fit in a piece of iron designed to hold the figure's extended arm in place. After that was done, the carving became more precise; chiseling brought out the details of the form, and finer details were finished with lighter tools. Finally, the arms were attached to the body with screws and the figure was painted and ready for delivery. It took the carver approximately a week's time to finish the figure.

Some of the cigar-store figures that were black include a jockey, a steamboat roustabout, and even a portrait of the black preacher Reverend Campbell. The famous detective Alan Pinkerton, who was President Lincoln's bodyguard during the Civil War, was the person who commissioned a carver to make Campbell's figure. Campbell had been hired by Pinkerton's to fill out their "freedom papers." His figure shows him dressed as Pinkerton suggested: in a long red coat with a carpetbag and umbrella.

THE FOLK ARTISTS

Steve Ashby was born in Fauquier County, Virginia, in 1907. After his wife died in 1962, he began making wood constructions, many of which had moving parts. He worked with a variety of materials and portrayed life as he knew it. He died in 1980.

David Butler, born in 1898, works in metal and tin, making whirligigs, trains, biblical scenes, and animals. He did not begin his work until he was hurt in a work-related accident late in life. He then began devoting all his time to "snipped tin" or cut, folded, and painted metal sculptures.

Originally from Louisiana, he was one of eight children. His father, Edward, was a carpenter and his mother was a missionary. His work has been shown at the New Orleans Museum of Art (1976) and was included in the exhibit and book "Black Folk Art in America 1930–1980."

Ulysses Davis was born in 1914. Davis's finest accomplishment is thought to be his carved busts of forty presidents. Each bust is carved from mahogany to show the likeness of the man and is signed with the president's name and dates of office.

Davis, a woodcarver extraordinaire, was one of eleven children, born and raised in Georgia. He is also the proprietor of Ulysses' Barber Shop.

Davis is known for his free-standing carved figures. One of the Crucifixion, entitled *Jesus on the Cross*, stands 40″ high and is held by the Kiah Museum. His work was included in "Missing Pieces: Georgia Folk Art 1770–1976," which toured major U.S. museums in 1976. He was also included in the exhibit and book "Black Folk Art in America 1930–1980."

William Dawson, born in 1901, is a sculptor who has shown his work at Chicago's Public Library, Phyllis Kind Gallery, Hyde Park Art Center, School of the Art Institute, and Museum of Contemporary Art. He was included in the exhibit and book "Black Folk Art in America 1930–1980."

What makes his success so amazing is the fact that he did not begin sculpting until after his retirement in the mid-sixties.

His subjects include religious stories (*Joseph in His Blue Robe*), current events (*Idi Amin Walking his Pet Pig*), and characters from folk tales. He has done totem poles and wood relief works. His figures have been carved and painted, and at times he adds varnish and glitter.

William Edmondson (1870–1951), one of the best-known black American folk artists, was recognized as an American artist as early as 1937 when he exhibited at the Museum of Modern Art. He worked exclusively in limestone, sculpting figures and animals with chisels he fashioned himself. One of these figures, *Little Lady*, was sold by Sotheby's in New York in 1982 for $14,950.

Although it is known that Edmondson's parents were slaves, the precise circumstances of his birth are not known.

His works have been shown at the Nashville Art Gallery (1941), Nashville Artist Guild (1951), Willard Gallery in New York (1964 and 1971), Tennessee Fine Arts Center at Cheekwood, Nashville (1964), Montclair, New Jersey, Art Museum (1975), and Tennessee State Museum in Nashville (1981). He

A group of counter-top figures made by Jacob Joyner of Mississippi. *Courtesy of Rose Fontanella; photo by Donald Vogt.*

Cigar store figure, approximately 2′ tall, by Jacob Joyner of Tupelo, Mississippi. A folk carver who worked during the 1920s and 1930s, Joyner also made life-size pieces. *Courtesy of Diane Higgin; photo by Donald Vogt.*

African boy apothecary trade sign, mid-nineteenth century. Wood and pottery, painted in polychrome with red coat, black-and-gold striped pants, black hair, brown hands and face. Pestle missing. *Courtesy of the Shelburne Museum, Shelburne, Vermont.*

Washerwoman whirligig by Steve Ashby. When wind blows the paddles, the woman's arms move up and down in a washing motion. *Collection of Gene and Linda Kangas; photo by Gene Kangas.*

was also included in the exhibit and book entitled "Black Folk Art in America 1930–1980."

Joshua Johnson was a self-taught ex-slave who was an active portrait painter during the years 1789–1825. He lived in Baltimore and in West Virginia and Virginia. Born about 1765, he died about 1830.

Some scholars have indicated that Johnson was a slave who was trained as a blacksmith. He advertised his services as a "self-taught painter" during the eighteenth century. We know him as the first black portraitist to win recognition in America.

He was believed to have served his painting apprenticeship under the Peale family or their contemporaries, and did most of his work between 1796 and 1824. His portraits were commissioned by Maryland's leading families when that occupation was inaccessible to black Americans.

His works include portraits of Mrs. John Moale and her granddaughter, the McCormick family, the Westwood children, Edward and Sarah Rutter, Mary McCurdy and daughters, and Mrs. West and Mary Ann West.

Only two black portraits have been attributed to Johnson. Because of the times during which he lived, he had to rely on white patronage. Blacks did not have the money or the social position to warrant portraits.

Johnson's subjects often hold objects that identify their business or hobby. His style is evident in his brushwork as well as his treatment of clothing, hair, and accessories.

The first time his work was exhibited was in 1948 at Baltimore's Peale Museum. His paintings were then given a long rest before being shown at the Metropolitan Museum in New York in 1961. After that time, he has been exhibited in most of the major museums of the United States.

Auction prices for Johnson's paintings have reached six figures and higher during the last couple of years, causing a resurgence of interest in the artist. There are collections of his works in the Museum of Early Southern Decorative Arts in Winston-Salem, North Carolina, as well as the Frick Gallery and Metropolitan Museum of Art in New York.

The Abby Aldrich Rockefeller Folk Art Center in Williamsburg, Virginia, was recently awarded a $28,000 grant to research the life—and the meaning of that life—of Joshua Johnson. Perhaps through their research and consultations with experts, we will come to know Joshua Johnson and his works more intimately than we do now.

Sister Gertrude Morgan (1900–1980). Driven by a powerful belief in God and a determination to fulfill His purpose for her, Sister Gertrude Morgan produced a number of drawings that depict biblical prophecies or her understanding of them. She was a painter, talented singer, and preacher who believed she was to become the bride of Christ. Her work reveals her exuberance through the use of bright and vibrant colors. Her writings and gospel lyrics were often repeated in her drawings and paintings.

Her work was exhibited widely during her lifetime, including exhibits at the Borenstein Gallery, New Orleans (1970), Louisiana Arts and Science Center, Baton Rouge (1972), and New Orleans Jazz and Heritage Fair (1974). She has also been included in such exhibits as "Dimensions in Black" at the La Jolla, California, Museum of Contemporary Art (1970), "Louisiana Folk Paintings" at the Museum of American Folk Art, New York (1973), and "Black Folk Art in America 1930–1980."

Elijah Pierce, a prolific woodcarver born in 1892, began his life as the son of an ex-slave in northeastern Mississippi. Elijah did not follow in the footsteps of his father, a farmer. Instead, he preferred the life of a wanderer, barber, and preacher.

He was married three times. His third wife joined him during the period of his life when he traveled throughout the Midwest giving sermons—he was awarded a preacher's license by the Mt. Zion Baptist Church—and using his carvings to illustrate them.

During the early 1970s his works were shown in solo exhibitions throughout the Midwest as well as in New York. In 1973 he was awarded first prize at the International Meeting of Naive Art in Zagreb, Yugoslavia. He was included in the exhibit and book "Black Folk Art in America 1930–1980" and has been the subject of films and magazine articles.

William Matthew Prior (1806–1873) was born in Bath, Maine, the son of Sarah Bryant and Matthew Prior. He took up painting in 1816 after his father was lost at sea.

Prior also supported himself by doing ornamental painting and japanning. He married Rosamund Clark Hamblen in Bath in 1828. Her brothers were also artists.

In 1840, the Priors and Hamblens moved to Boston and began working as a team producing portraits. Between 1842 and 1844 they lived in East Boston. Prior was a Millerite, which may explain why he sympathetically painted such subjects as the preacher Reverend Lawson and his wife.

Bill Traylor (1854–1947). A photograph of Traylor shows an elderly, bearded man whose eyes are forceful and piercing. He sits at a table with a pencil held in each hand, a drawing on the table in front of him. The hands are large, working hands. His figure and countenance do not appear to be that of a man close to ninety years old, yet we know that to be the case because Bill Traylor did not begin to draw until 1939 at the age of eighty-five.

He was born a slave in Alabama, remained on the farm where he was born until he was eighty-four, then moved to Montgomery, where he held a job until rheumatism forced him to quit. His drawings are geometric stick figures, usually showing people in action or at work. His work, like that of many folk artists, was drawn from life.

Traylor seemed surprised when people bought his drawings. He must have been even more shocked when his art was shown in Montgomery at an art center called New South in 1940 and in 1941 at the Fieldston School in New York City. It was also shown after his death in a New York gallery as well as in an exhibition circulated by the Southern Arts Federation in 1981–1982 entitled "Southern Works on Paper." Traylor's works and biography were included in the exhibit and book "Black Folk Art in America 1930–1980."

George White (1903–1970) was a man of many professions: an adventurer, lawman, and artist. His work *Emancipation*

Portrait of Barbara Baker Murphy, wife of a sea captain, by Joshua Johnson, oil on canvas, ca. 1810. Part of "Sharing Traditions: Five Black Artists in 19th century America." *Courtesy of National Museum of American Art; transfer from National Museum of African Art, gift of Sol and Lillian Koffler.*

PRICE GUIDE—FOLK ART

It should be noted at the onset that folk art is just as difficult to price as fine art. Although some folk art is not one-of-a-kind, most of it is, and to be able to determine what you might pay for an item is not always an easy task. If you love a piece of folk art and can't live without it, no price is too high. If you're buying for resale, you have to know what the market in your area will stand. One good thing that I can see with folk art is that its popularity does not seem to be declining. I, for one, have never had a problem selling a piece of folk art—at any price.

House is included in the pieces displayed at the National Museum of American Art of the Smithsonian Institution in Washington, D.C.

His carved wood reliefs are detailed glimpses into American life. He painted his figures in oil, sometimes used a mixed-media construction, but whatever the formula, his scenes were realistic down to the smallest detail. His sculptures show scenes from his life as a Southern black man, as well as his life as a Texas outdoorsman. They are executed sensitively and even humorously.

Other carvings are housed in New York galleries, the Waco Creative Art Center in Texas—where he received a solo exhibition in 1975—as well as the Smithsonian. He was included in the exhibition and book "Black Folk Art in America 1930–1980."

DESCRIPTION	APPROXIMATE PRICE
Ashtray, standing, wood, black butler, 1890s	$1,200–$1,500
Ceramic head, old black man with beard, semibald, possibly made from cinders or black clay, 5″	$75–$135
Counter piece for minstrel show, Ohio, 1910–1920, "The Banjo Man"	$6,000–$10,000
Doll, stuffed cloth, dressed in red and white, stitched eyes and eyebrows, applied nose and mouth, mint condition, ca. 1850, 18″	$3,000–$3,500
Figure, concrete, boy with watermelon	$45–$60
Figure, wooden, twentieth century, full length, black man dressed as porter, upper torso with working music box, outstretched arms holds removable copper ashtray, 35″	$2,000–$2,800

The Reverend W. Lawson, oil on canvas, painted by William Prior. *Courtesy of the Shelburne Museum, Shelburne, Vermont.*

Mrs. Nancy Lawson, oil on canvas, painted May 11, 1843, by William Prior. *Courtesy of the Shelburne Museum, Shelburne, Vermont.*

Figurine, black native, polychrome, 21¼″ .... $400–$750

Measuring stick, hickory, 81½″ × 15″ × 11 ″ base, bar slides up and down pole with carved measuring lines. Found in a tunnel beneath the Lankford House in Somerset, Maryland, reportedly used by the abolitionist Patty Cannon to smuggle slaves .... $575–$875

Needlepoint piece, male and female dancing figures, "We's Free"* ....$475–$1,000

Pressed wood figure, woman wearing apron, hands on hips, 6″, ca. 1935....................... $52–$70

Primitive painting, unsigned, young girl, ribbon in hair, ca. 1890 .... $195–$350

Quilt, made of homspun pieces, 1820–1840, Georgia .... $195–$275

*One will see a number of these "samplers" during the period that one collects black Americana. They are as different in size, condition, and craftsmanship as were the people who made them. Perhaps it was the "in" thing to do in order to celebrate their freedom, or, as has been suggested to me, we may be dealing with a "repro" of the highest quality. They cover a wide range of prices and you will rarely find two that are the same price as well as condition, quality of workmanship, and size.

Redware, figure of buxom Mammy, Southern "offhand" piece from last quarter of nineteenth century, 1″ thick, extremely heavy .... $1,000–$1,500

Sampler, cross-stitch, 7½″ × 8½″, ca. 1890, woman and man outside house.......................$695–$1,000

Smoke stand, painted metal, black man in butler's uniform, holding ashtray.............. $110–$160

Statue, watermelon scene, chalk, 15″.............. $135–$175

String puppet, made by American Crayon Co., Sandusky, Ohio/New York, 14½″ tall, original box, red-and-white suit, white top hat .... $175–$195

Watercolor, primitive, black man trying to kiss white man, signed H.S.S., 2½″ × 3″, ca. 1830 .... $395–$500

Watercolor, 3½″ × 4½″, original frame, black woman with large plaid skirt, 1840–1860... $575–$750

Whirligig, windmill, black Mammy, scrubbing clothes, 10¾″...................................... $350–$500

Woodcarving, black boy holding watermelon, painted, 5½″... $40–$95

"I hain't seen nuffin ob yer chickens," oil on canvas, ca. 1870. *Collection of Joseph W. and Nathan Wood; photo by Donald Vogt.*

A hand-painted standing ashtray, made during the turn of the century. *Collection of Joseph W. and Nathan Wood; photo by Donald Vogt.*

Charcoal drawing of man with elbow on his knee, signed in lower right corner "Jean Erskler." *Courtesy of Rose Fontanella; photo by Donald Vogt.*

"Samuel Rastus Sweeney," reputed to be the mascot of a nineteenth-century Mississippi riverboat. He is 39½" tall, stuffed with old chair stuffing from head to toe, and dressed in vintage children's clothing (including his leather shoes). His face and features are hand stitched, his tongue and teeth are wood. *Courtesy of collection of Gene and Linda Kangas; photos by Gene Kangas.*

A carved wooden folk art figure shows a black preacher with a whiskey bottle in one hand and a Bible in the other. *Anonymous private collection, courtesy of Ken and Ida Manko; photo by Donald Vogt.*

A carved pipe with an alligator eating a man, probably made to satisfy the tourist trade since it is unfortunately not one-of-a-kind. *Courtesy of Bonner's Barn; photo by Robideau Studios.*

A life-size carving of a black woman with child on hip and begging bowl at her feet is in wonderful warm shades of mahogany. *Courtesy of Bonner's Barn; photo by Robideau Studios.*

An architectural piece, a pediment of a column for the side of a building, shows a Negro slave woman in a toga. *Courtesy of Bonner's Barn; photo by Robideau Studios.*

Old Man, a sculpture by Ben Heller, utilizes several different kinds of nut shells, thistles, and wire. *Courtesy of Martin and Anne Ellman; photo by Donald Vogt.*

A nineteenth-century wood carving of a black head is thought to have been used as a target for balls in a shooting gallery. *Courtesy of the Shelburne Museum, Shelburne, Vermont.*

77

THOMAS DAY, CABINET MAKER,

RETURNS his thanks for the patronage he has received, and wishes to inform his friends and the public that he has on hand, and intends keeping, a handsome supply of *Mahogony, Walnut and Stained FURNITURE,* the most fashionable, and common BED STEADS, &c. which he would be glad to sell very low. All orders in his line, in Repairing, Varnishing, &c. will be thankfully received and punctuallo attended to.
Jan. 17.   38

P. H. & R. W. THOMAS,
HAVING connected themselves in the practice and sale of MEDICINES, of.

Advertisement, January 17, 1827, announcing the opening of Thomas Day's shop. *Photo courtesy of North Carolina Museum of History.*

Milton, Feb 1858.

NOTIE.

THE subscriber wishes his friends to know he has still a large assortment of fine **Cabinet Furniture,** on hand ... eties of the most Fashionable and durable mahogany, rosewood, and walnut house-hold **FURNITURE** used in the most fashionable Parlors, and also among housekeepers of all circumstances.
French Sofas,
    Chairs,
        Bedsteads of all kinds,
           Bureaus with mirrors,
              Mahogany, Walnut, and Oak Extension Tables,
                Atayshas of all kinds are on hand. Persons wanting Furniture will find it to their interest to call and examine. Money is greatly desired by the proprietor, and for cash good bargains may be expected.
For all **BURIAL** purposes full and ready accommodation is ever at hand to carry to any distance at very short notice and with all necessary care and attention.
We invite and solicit our customers to consult their own interest, and we shall not lack support.   THO'S DAY.
Milnto, march 1858.   tf

February 1858 advertisement featuring Thomas Day's specialties. *Photo courtesy of North Carolina Museum of History.*

Cradle made by Thomas Day and currently owned by Dr. and Mrs. Edwin J. Harvie. *Photo courtesy of North Carolina Museum of History.*

8

Furniture

When I first came upon the name of Thomas Day, it surprised me that so little had been written about a man who, in his day, made great achievements both in the North Carolina furniture industry and in furthering his own career. What was most unusual is that much of the information that I found on Day did not jibe. One book said he was born in Jamaica, another said his birthplace was the British West Indies island of Nevis, and yet another placed his birth somewhere in North Carolina. One source said he was married twice; another mentioned only one marriage.

I was ready to give up the job of researching this elusive character when I had the good fortune to discover that his furniture was held by the North Carolina Museum of History and that they possessed a great deal of information about him.

It is through their literature that I discovered the truths and mysteries of the furniture maker Thomas Day and it is to the North Carolina Museum of History that the following chapter is dedicated—with many thanks.

THOMAS DAY—FURNITURE MAKER AND EXTRAORDINARY BLACK MAN

According to the 1850 and 1860 federal censuses for North Carolina, both Day and his mother, who was a resident of his household at the time of the census, were born in Virginia. The approximate birth year given for Day was 1801.

His mother was given her freedom in North Carolina, and sent Day to Boston and Washington for three years to study wood carving.

His arrival in Caswell County, North Carolina, came at a time when Milton, the town where he settled, was in a state of rapid growth and development. The center of the county's tobacco economy, Milton was surrounded by upper-class families whose needs for services helped the town and its merchants develop quickly.

Though some reports claim that Day's first venture into the furniture business began on his parents' farm outside Milton, the truth is that we do not know where Day began. But in 1827 he bought a lot on Main Street in Milton for $550 cash, which apparently became his new shop. A January 17, 1827, notice that he had set up shop gave no address, leaving one to believe that the people of the town knew exactly where the shop was.

In 1830, Day traveled to Virginia to marry Aquilla Wilson, a free woman of Halifax. Because North Carolina's laws forbade blacks to travel from state to state, Day was accused of breaking the law. The immigration laws, put into effect because the plantation owners wanted total control over their slaves' whereabouts, also forbade his wife from legally residing in North Carolina.

Day took a stand and threatened to move to Virginia to be with his wife. Because of his respected position in the community, the citizens of Milton petitioned the state legislature to make an exception in Day's case. Exceptions were often made to exempt talented blacks from the impact of the law, but the fact that state action was taken shows just how favorable a position Day held in the town.

The petition declared Day to be a "first rate workman, a remarkably sober, steady and industrious man, a high minded, good and valuable citizen, possessing a handsome property in this town," and was made even stronger by a personal testimony from Romulus Sanders, the state's attorney general.

In 1830, the General Assembly passed the petition after a second reading and welcomed Aquilla Wilson into the state.

Day's position in the town grew stronger over the next forty years. He purchased stock in the bank, bought a second piece of property on Main Street, and in 1848 purchased the Union Tavern, which he converted into a residence and miniature factory where both white apprentices and black slaves were taught the furniture trade. The building, later named the Yellow Tavern, has since become a historical landmark.

In the 1850 industrial census, Day is noted to have had a $5,800 capital investment in a business which employed twelve workers." The total capital investment by North Carolina carpenters and builders was noted to be "$20,875 with a total employment of 80 hands." It doesn't take a mathematical genius to realize how strong Day's business was at that time.

Day's talents were many. He retailed and wholesaled furniture from his shop to such merchants as John Wilson and Richard Smith, as well as finishing custom orders for Governor David S. Reid and a number of prominent North Carolina families.

Day also did house carpentry, some of which is well documented by the University of North Carolina at Chapel Hill, even though the buildings that housed his unusual interior carpentry are no longer standing. His newel posts are extremely innovative and his sense of style and grace clearly comes through as his own, not as copies of what was popular during that time. One such newel post was made for the Holmes Hunt house, a residence about four miles outside of Milton. The elaborate curves and twists of the post suggest a free-form style unlike any other of the day and cause viewers to exclaim over its beauty. You know the wood gleams and must be like silk to the touch even though you are just admiring a black-and-white photo.

Day did work for the University of North Carolina's library, even though his bid was higher than others entered in competition for the job. According to legend, his bid was accepted because the university's president believed Day's work to be the best in the area.

Through letters and billing, we see that Day was a strong personality, a man who believed in his work so strongly that he did not back down when questioned about his prices, nor let his designs be changed to meet someone else's whim. He did not allow himself or his creations to be compromised in any way.

Though Day was exempted from the law in order to marry Aquilla Wilson, he was still bound under all other laws regarding Negroes, of which there were many in that turbulent era before the Civil War. Despite that fact, Day and his family maintained a respectable position in the community, were active members of the Milton Presbyterian Church, and even sent their three children, Mary Ann, Devereaux, and Thomas Jr., to Massachusetts's Wilbraham Academy to complete their education. His children went on to become prominent members and pioneers in the black community. It is said that Devereaux went to South America, Mary Ann got married, and Thomas Jr. took over his father's business, running it until he sold it in 1871.

As with his birthdate, Day's date of death is undocumented, but tradition states it to be 1861. When he died, he was reputed to be the wealthiest free Negro in North Carolina—worth about $100,000.

Day also left his legacy of beautifully carved chairs, tables, footstools, bureaus, and desks, made from walnut or imported East Indian mahogany. His furniture is currently on display in the North Carolina Historical Museum in Raleigh, North Carolina, as well as being held in the following private collections.

PRIVATE COLLECTIONS OF DAY FURNITURE

• *Lucille Reid Flagg* of Eden, North Carolina, holds furniture descended directly from Governor Reid. Her collection includes a sofa in the Louis XV revival style, as well as tables and side chairs.

• *Mary Roane Harvie* (Mrs. Edwin James) of Danville, Virginia, owns furniture made by Day that was originally purchased by Dr. Nathaniel Moore Roan of Yanceyville and has descended through the Harvie Family. Her collection includes a mahogany whatnot that is representative of Day's best work, a sideboard, rocker, nest of tables, and footstool.

• *Dr. and Mrs. Edwin J. Harvie* of Danville, Virginia, own another part of the Dr. Roan purchase, which includes an impressive extension table made in three pieces in mahogany, a cradle, and a sleigh bed.

• *Mabel J. Hunt* (Mrs. Holmes) of Ringold, Virginia, has pieces of Day's furniture that have descended through the Hunt family for six generations. The furniture stands in the same house for which it was originally crafted and consists of a secretary, wardrobes, bureaus, and an elaborately carved cottage bed.

• *W. S. Angle*, the former mayor of Milton, North Carolina, has been collecting Day furniture and ephemera for years. His collection includes an unusual piano stool, a rocking chair, and a rather plain (by Day's standards) settee.

• *Mrs. Hines Hatchett* of Yanceyville, North Carolina, holds furniture crafted by Day that has been in her family since about 1850. The pieces include a marble-top washstand, a mahogany-veneer wardrobe and sideboard, and a charming rural secretary.

• *Cecelia Reid Scott Hester* (Mrs. William C.) of Reidsville, North Carolina, owns furniture that was purchased from R. P. Richardson by attorney Hugh R. Scott. Richardson bought the pieces from R. W. Lawson. They include rococo revival sofas, balloon-back lady's and gentleman's chairs, and side chairs.

• *Edwin Monroe Lynch* of Hillsborough, North Carolina, has pieces that were originally bought by Ezekiel Jones of Caswell County (Lynch's great uncle) and were passed through Lynch's mother to him. The pieces include a sofa, side chair, dropleaf writing table, and Louis XV sofa.

OTHER BLACK FURNITURE MAKERS

There were other black furniture makers during Day's time. However, because of the white slave owners' fear that black craftsmen would take over their business, the slaves' work was kept quiet and few received credit for the work they accomplished.

However, Durtevil Barjon of New Orleans was another black furniture maker whose work was moderately well known and sought after in the Delta region of Louisiana. In the city directory for New Orleans dated 1822, Barjon was listed as a "free man of color." In 1823, he advertised his shop on Royal Street in New Orleans and his ability to make furniture and looking glasses. There is not much more information written about him.

PRICE GUIDE—FURNITURE

After extensive research with little to no result, I have concluded that there was little made in the way of furniture by slaves. I have "discovered" one black man named Thomas Day, who, through hard work and adherence to the laws of the community, made furniture of a high quality in his own factory. He is, however, the only furniture maker of any significance on whom I could find information. Because most of his pieces are in museums and historical places of interest, there are no prices available.

Mahogany secretary owned by Mrs. Holmes Hunt and passed down through the Hunt family. *Photo courtesy of North Carolina Museum of History.*

Lady's and gentleman's balloon-back chairs made by Thomas Day and now owned by Cecelia Reid Scott Hester of Reidsville, North Carolina. *Photo courtesy of North Carolina Museum of History.*

Thomas Day whatnot, made of mahogany, owned by Edwin Monroe Lynch of Hillsborough, North Carolina. *Photo courtesy of North Carolina Museum of History.*

The only other information I can give you about furniture is that a number of "slave" chairs have been found and are located all over the country, most notably in the Slave Trade Museum in New Orleans. The chairs have been described as heavily carved, or as having chains from the arms and around the back of the chair—supposedly to keep the slave in place during an auction. These chairs have interesting and, in some cases, horrifying histories, and it seems that when such a chair is sold, its history is passed on to the next owner, to be kept alive for eternity. Perhaps they are the one item, along with their story, that will forever remind us of the cruelties and abnormalities of slave life.

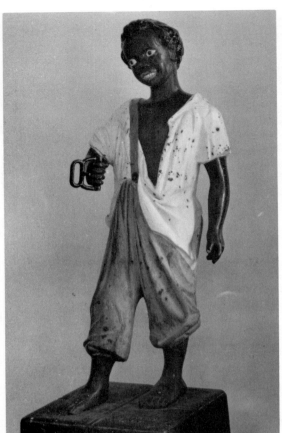

Stable-boy hitching post, polychromed cast-iron figure standing on a bale of cotton, signed J. W. Fiske, New York. *Photograph courtesy of James Abbe, Jr.*

Black butler andirons, ca. 1840, made in Georgia. *Collection of Joseph W. and Nathan Wood; photo by Donald Vogt.*

Jockey, polychromed cast-iron hitching post. *Courtesy of Bonner's Barn; photo by Robideau Studios.*

Cast-iron miniature jockey hitching post, approximately 2″. *Courtesy of Basia Kirschner; photo by Donald Vogt.*

9

Iron

ARCHITECTURAL IRONWORK

It has often been argued by craftsmen and connoisseurs alike that the lacy grilles, lunettes, and balconies of New Orleans were not made by slaves. Or perhaps, the arguers admit, they *were* done by slaves but those slaves must have had European supervisors because the work is too intricate, the wrought iron too beautifully and sensitively done. Yet the argument *for* the Negro craftsman is handily won because all skilled trades and crafts were monopolized by blacks until after 1830, when immigration resulted in the new Americans pushing into areas that had been, for years, areas of black craftsmanship.

New Orleans was founded in 1718 by French settlers. Ceded to Spain in 1763, Louisiana was under Spanish rule until 1801. The buildings that remain standing from that period reflect a Latin architectural influence that has a beauty and grace all its own. It only takes common sense to realize that the Spanish people who inhabited this area wanted to have their homes look like the ones they left behind.

Louisiana plantations all had blacksmiths in order to make tools, horseshoes, and other iron necessities, and the smiths were indeed black. Often a talented blacksmith would be sent to New Orleans to work and his wages would be sent back to the plantation owner. Thus the argument that the slaves did *not* do the ironwork in the South is lost. They *were* the ironworkers, and were more than likely taught by the people whose houses were decorated with iron railings and the like to make those decorative accents in a Spanish manner.

Being sent to work in New Orleans often was to the slave's advantage. If the wrought-iron worker chose to buy his freedom, he need only put in some overtime to save toward the fee he would be charged for his freedom—usually $500.

The ironworker/blacksmith of that time was blessed with the luck that gave him unlimited opportunities to show off his talent. Everyone needed ironwork in some shape or form. The mansions of New Orleans with their marvelously intricate balconies, railings, courtyards, and architectural additives were the accidental result of the fire of 1788, which burned the city down. Forced to start anew, the French and Spanish entrepreneurs of the city hired Negro artists to provide the work needed to complete grandiose houses to compete with the ones they had left behind in their native lands.

The gentleman or his architect would show the slave/blacksmith an engraving of work done in his homeland and ask the slave to produce something similar. The Negro artisan then went about the task of interpreting the curves of rococo styling or the clean, strong lines of the classic revival style into smithing terms. Thus, the designs one finds in the Vieux Carré section of New Orleans combine the grace and modeling of the Old World while ever so subtly giving us a glimpse of the black artisan's style.

The lacy grillwork on the houses in the South was liberally used and seemed to suit the area's warm climate. Though most buildings were privately owned, they housed businesses on the raised pavement beside the street, called a banquette. The living quarters were entered through a paved passageway, more than likely framed by wrought-iron gates. Once in the living quarters, the ironwork became even more ornamental. Galleries, sometimes running continuously from one building to the next down the entire street, were made to offer protection from the sun and showers.

The lacy ironwork done by slaves in the South can also be found in the older, well-established cities such as New York, Boston, Philadelphia, Baltimore, Georgetown, and Charlestown.

A letter written by Mrs. Basil Hall in 1828 showed her delight with New Orleans's "old Continental aspect . . . [a] lively, French tone heard in the streets . . . houses with queerly-shaped high roofs and iron balconies" looking "deliciously cool for summer use."

The Ursuline convent, erected in 1727, houses the oldest examples of wrought-iron work in New Orleans. All the ironwork at the convent was wrought by "brute Africans."

Each blacksmith had his own favorite design. Sometimes the delicately turned iron had to be heated as many as eight times in order to bend it into the required pattern. Names of the patterns—"widow's mite," "shell," "diamond," "tulip"—are reminiscent of quilt patterns.

In 1857 it was noted that iron production in the United States was secondary only to that of England.

The rapid growth of the iron industry was largely due to the popularity of the metal. It could be made into every conceivable design and shape—and at a relatively small cost.

Cast iron was used as columns on buildings, as porches, lawn furniture, doorstops, radiator covers, stoves, and match safes. It was used for so many things in the 1860s and 1870s that enthusiasm for cast iron was soon dubbed "ferromania."

Contrary to popular belief, most of a smithy's work was done on cold iron by file and saw. The roaring fire, the worker with his sleeves rolled up, sweat oozing from every pore in his body, his muscles bulging with exertion, is the mental picture one gets of an early ironworker. Yet in all actuality, the heat was applied only in the preliminary stages.

Ironwork has been considered the first Afro-American art. It was a craft that ran a forty-year course, allowing the first unmistakable talents of the Negro, who had been plucked from his native home, to show through. And the talent *did* speak out, clearly and boldly.

If the period of cast iron had lasted longer, we might have been rewarded with another century of wonders made by Negro blacksmiths. But progress persists, and the black ironworker ceased to provide decorative accents to graceful Southern mansions years before the Civil War awarded slaves their freedom.

OTHER IRON COLLECTIBLES

ANDIRONS

Andirons are the oldest of fireplace utensils, having been produced since the late Iron Age. They are horizontal iron bars fitted with a guard at each end used to keep logs from rolling off. The guard was often made in the form of a statue or other decoration.

The andirons produced in America until the early 1900s were generally less ornate than the French and English styles. A number of American andirons were made in the form of black persons or characters. The most commonly seen are jockeys, but sailors, Mammy and Pappy forms, and other "personalities" can also be found.

This type of andiron was usually made in the South, at the same foundries where slaves worked to design iron balustrades and railings for Southern homes. Though the early to middle 1800s was the period when most andirons were manufactured, one can find prime examples of these decorative fireplace pieces made during the latter part of the century as well.

When buying andirons, be wary of any with brightly colored paint. If the andirons were used in a fireplace, as originally intended, the paint should be fairly faded and chipped by now. Any andirons with bright paint were probably repainted at one time and should be treated like any other repaired antique: that is, the price should reflect the repairs.

DOORSTOPS

Doorstops were invented about 1775 to keep open doors that incorporated the newly invented rising butt type of door hinge. Although the first examples were molded in earthenware, other doorstops were cast in iron, bronze, and brass. Manufacturers began making doorstops in fanciful shapes, the earliest being bells, Staffordshire figures, and Shakespearean characters.

Doorstops—or door porters—became familiar objects in Victorian homes. They often took the form of celebrities of the time, or animals, or inanimate objects such as Punch and Judy. The black Mammy doorstop remains one of the most collectible.

The most common doorstop material was metal, which was usually cast with a flat, hollow back. However, some of the early examples were cast in the round. Lacquered brass doorstops were popular until about 1850, and cast-iron from about 1820 on. When production of doorstops increased, the makers began to add paint or a bronzed finish as extra decoration.

Because of the recent vogue for collecting them, prices of doorstops are now at an all-time high. Magazines such as *Country Living* and *Colonial Homes* have devoted full-length articles to the subject and there are already a number of books on the market covering the area of doorstop collecting. Since interest in these items is so high, one must begin to be cautious about the price being asked for a stop, its condition, and whether or not it is a reproduction.

Fortunately, the market has not yet been flooded with repros, but you can expect that it soon will be. As in the past with items such as iron banks, companies try to take advantage of current trends by making new examples of antique collectibles. Certainly the new items fill a need for those of us who don't care to spend the money these pieces are currently commanding. However, if you are looking for something that will become more valuable as time goes by, reproductions are not the way to go. Some of us, antiques dealers in particular, do not want the new copies strictly because they are new. However, if you want a decorative accent and don't want to pay over $50 for a stop, the new ones do serve a purpose.

The most common black doorstop is the Mammy. She is seen in many different colors and sizes and can be found at just about any antiques show. Reproductions of the Mammy stop are also surfacing, usually brightly painted in shades of red and blue. Once you have seen a few antique doorstops and are aware that the paint on the old stops chips and fades with the passage of time, the new doorstops will be immediately recognizable as fakes.

Besides the Mammy, there are many other black doorstops. Some are pretty rare, but if you hunt diligently, you may be able to find the butler doorstop or the child eating watermelon. There are also jockeys, black musicians, and other figures to add to your black doorstop collection.

HITCHING POSTS

The hitching post, used to secure visitors' horses, was first made during the 1860s. When a farmer drove into town, he looked for a hitching post because the post was the mark of a good store.

Companies such as J. W. Fiske or Mott Ironworks made most of the posts supplied in the horse-and-buggy era.

The cast-iron post succeeded the wrought-iron one. The earliest posts were usually topped with a horse's head that held a ring for the reins.

Human figures were introduced as hitching posts during the mid-nineteenth century when iron foundries began to explore new fields. Jockeys, Sambos, footmen, and stable boys were some of the figures representing black people. The jockeys and footmen wore brightly painted clothes, and those who could afford them placed them in front of their homes. The hitching post became a status symbol of sorts. The better the post, the better the home it represented.

Although the black slave boy is probably the most common of all posts, it is not the oldest. The 25″ "darky" hitching post is considered to be the oldest. "Darky" is dapperly dressed in spats, cap, checkered vest, and squarish pants. On a wood or concrete base, the figure stands with one hand outstretched and the other in its pocket. Two or three variations of this figure can be found, each slightly different according to age.

The jockey is another familiar form of the hitching post. Usually 46″ to 48″ high, the jockey was the elite of the posts, being found outside hotels, estates, restaurants, and other places of gentlemanly leisure.

Hitching posts make an interesting addition to a home. Besides guarding the front lawn or driveway, they can be placed in a hallway, at the foot of the stairs, or even beside the fireplace.

Though condition is always important to a collector, hitching posts should not be expected to retain all their original paint. Since they were an outdoor object, they are often chipped, faded, and pitted. Don't let that concern you. However, do watch for newly repainted pieces—bright whites in the eyes are always a giveaway—and expect a price adjustment when such repairs have been made.

PRICE GUIDE—IRON OBJECTS

DESCRIPTION	APPROXIMATE PRICE
Andirons, black butlers, ca. 1820, made in Georgia	$1,200–$1,500
Andirons, black sailor boys, ca. 1820, made in Georgia	$1,500–$2,500
Andirons, cast iron, black youths in plumed skirt, leggings	$400–$600
Andirons, figural, black man and woman, Pennsylvania, ca. 1830, 16½″	$1,200–$1,600
Ashtray, standing, butler, red and black with brass trays, 34″ tall	$250–$400
Automaton clock, Negress, ca. 1870, 16¼″	$835–$890
Black boy and mule cart, boy whips mule, cast iron	$595–$725
Boot scraper, black, child	$195–$250
Bottle opener, alligator biting black man, cast iron	$30–$50
Bottle opener, black face	$65–$75
Bottle opener, figural, black minstrel, 3½″ × 4½″ × 1½″	$75–$95
Bottle opener, Negro head, figural, cast iron, 3¾″ × 4¼″	$65–$75
Broom holder, black boy, barefoot, red suit, cast iron, 5″	$95–$105
Broom holder, figural, black man	$155–$175
Doorstop, Aunt Jemima	$65–$95
Doorstop, black boy, hitching post, ring in hand, 11½″	$45–$75
Doorstop, black butler	$90–$125
Doorstop, Mammy, blue dress, 8½″	$145–$180
Doorstop, Mammy, full figure, 5½″	$85–$105
Figurine, Aunt Jemima, original paint, 9″	$75–$110
Figurine, black stable boy, ragged trousers, polychrome, 49″	$1,045–$1,200
Figurine, Mammy, 2½″	$40–$60
Figurine, slave boy, running, 30″	$325–$475
Jockey hitching post, miniature cast iron, 1″ tall	$130–$150
Mask, 8″ face, features of black man, four holes (possibly used to tie the mask around the head), makes head bow when in place. (obedience mask?), ca. 1840	$425–$575
Match holder, black boys and watermelon, pot metal, 3″	$50–$60
Pan, frying, Mammy, miniature	$10–$15
Pencil sharpener, black minstrel	$45–$75
String holder, black man's head, signed Fredericksburg Art	$40–$60
String holder, Mammy	$11–$25
Water faucet handle, Negro's head, figural	$75–$95

Aunt Jemima in iron, 3″, shows lots of wear. *Courtesy of Jeanie Ohle; photo by Donald Vogt.*

California Pottery salt and pepper shakers have a white background and black polka dots. *Courtesy of Judy Posner; photo by Donald Vogt.*

10

Kitchen Collectibles

Things that belong in the kitchen—salt and pepper shakers, cookie jars, condiment sets—are what most people think of first when they think of black Americana. This is probably the easiest area of black Americana to collect because the pieces are accessible, affordable—and usable. Just about every black Americana dealer or collector whom we visited had at least one or two pieces that could be considered "kitchen collectibles."

This area of collecting is as wide and interesting as its objects are colorful. Although some of you may consider certain advertising pieces to fall into this category (and I tend to agree), I have kept the advertising pieces in their own chapter (Chapter 1) and more information may be obtained there.

When collecting items for the kitchen, if one is to keep in the black Americana frame of mind, one must be careful. Quite a few of the later kitchen pieces were made in Japan. I may even have made the mistake of including some photographs of Japanese-made articles. If so, I apologize. I have researched those items on which I could find information and have not used any that were marked "Made in Japan" or were obviously Japanese.

I wrestled with the idea of including "Occupied Japan" items, reasoning that they were made for the American market, but have decided that there was already an abundance of such articles made in the United States and there was no need to include those made in other countries. Perhaps they will be listed in a later book.

I must thank a number of dealers and collectors for their contributions to this chapter. In particular, Judy Posner for her fabulous collection of cookie jars in every shape, size, and description; Rose Fontanella for her unusual pieces (as well as for her help in every other category in the book)—Rose's collection surpassed most of those we saw; and Dakota Sands, whose collection of kitchen items was displayed lovingly and thoughtfully in her tiny apartment.

TYPES OF KITCHEN COLLECTIBLES

CONDIMENT SETS

These sets, sometimes designed to fit a specific advertising campaign—such as Aunt Jemima—were made of pottery, plastic, and china. You are lucky if you find a complete set as they were often put into everyday use and certain pieces were used more than others.

Sugar and creamer sets, often a part of condiment sets, are found alone and priced separately. If you look hard enough, you may find the rest of the set they originally matched.

COOKBOOKS

Cookbooks in the black tradition are noticeable by the front-cover illustrations or by the inherently black (or Southern) recipes they contain. It is worth your while collecting these books for the recipes alone; putting them into your black Americana collection comes second.

Though not always easy to find, the cookbooks are usually reasonably priced and make a nice addition to a shelf full of black kitchen collectibles.

COOKIE JARS

Cookie jars, which have been made from the early 1930s and continue to be made today, are very popular with collectors. Most common of the cookie jars is the Nelson McCoy version of Mammy. Made from 1940 to 1957, the Mammy sports a small head wrapped in a red bandana. She wears a voluminous white skirt with the word "cookies" emblazoned on the front. The first edition of this jar sported the phrase "Dem Cookies Sho' Do Taste Good" around the bottom of her skirt.

Many cookie jars now available have lost quite a bit of paint due to heavy use as well as the fact that since the piece was enameled after it was fired the color did not have durability.

Another cookie jar that is fairly rare is McCoy's 1939 Mammy with Basket of Cauliflowers. This jar was produced in limited quantities and was hand-painted over the glaze. Again, very few are found with the paint intact.

Unfortunately, the most attractive of McCoy cookie jars, a Mammy and black chef shoulder to shoulder, was never put into production.

Weller Pottery produced a Mammy cookie jar in 1938 that was part of a set consisting of a cookie jar, covered sugar bowl, creamer, batter bowl, teapot, and syrup jug. A set in mint condition, if you could find one, would be worth somewhere around $2,000.

Aunt Jemima spice set, six pieces with shelf, all original. Spice pieces are 3″ tall, salt and pepper 5″ tall. *Courtesy of Malinda Saunders; photo by Donald Vogt.*

Cookbook entitled *Aunt Caroline's Dixieland Recipes. Courtesy of Valerie Bertrand Collection; photo by Donald Vogt.*

A Weller pottery kitchen set of teapot, cookie jar, batter bowl, and syrup pitcher is rare and expensive. Missing from the photograph are the creamer and sugar. *Courtesy of Judy Posner; photo by Donald Vogt.*

The Mosaic Mammy Cookie Jar was originally attributed to the Mosaic Tile Company or the Zanesville Art Tile Company but now has been tentatively attributed to the Zanesville Art Tile Company. The patent number was issued to "K. M. Gale of Zanesville, Ohio." The jar was shown in the *1944 Patent Yearbook* and entitled the Mosaic Mammy cookie jar.

A rare cookie jar, "Mammy with Cauliflowers," made by McCoy. As is often the case, the colors, applied after the glaze was put on, have not proved durable. *Courtesy of Judy Posner; photo by Donald Vogt.*

Note pad holder, ca. 1940, of painted plaster. Versions of this item were made of celluloid, composition, or molded plastic. *Courtesy of Malinda Saunders; photo by Donald Vogt.*

Chef and Mammy potholder wall hangers. Their clothes are white with red trim. *Courtesy of Dakota Sands; photo by Donald Vogt.*

GROCERY LIST AND NOTE PAD HOLDERS

Mammy figures with note pads attached to their skirts have been made in composition, pottery, rubber, celluloid, and plastic. The older the note pad holder, the higher the price, although the ones made of composition or rubber are notorious for being in bad shape. The prices of these items fluctuate so widely that I hesitated even adding them to the price list. My only advice is to buy the best example you can afford and to try to keep your buying price under $45. Anything over that amount is too high for an item this common.

The grocery list holders are often rectangular pieces of wood that may or may not have a pegboard of suggested grocery items below a hand-painted Mammy figure or face.

Made during the 1930s to 1950s, these items are still available and make a nice accent for a kitchen wall.

PLAQUES

Most plaques made in the figure of a black person were made as kitchen accents in the 1930s, 1940s, and 1950s. Although most are plaster or chalkware, I have encountered composition, rubber, wooden, and plastic examples. The most common kitchen plaques feature black children with umbrellas or children sharing watermelon.

Watch for damage, such as flaking paint, and broken pieces that have been glued back together. These pieces are common enough that you can afford to wait until you find one in excellent condition for your collection.

Most plaques are not marked with the maker's name, but should be marked with the country of origin if they are not American.

POTHOLDER HANGERS

Made of pottery, chalkware, rubber, or plastic, potholder hangers come in different styles including black children, black Mammy and chef, Aunt Jemima, and many others. They were made as kitchen accents during the 1930s to 1950s and are still easily found in garage sales and flea markets at reasonable prices.

If the potholder hanger is an early one, expect the paint to be chipped and worn. This is not a concern if you are paying a small amount of money for the piece. If you are paying top dollar at an antique show, however, think twice before giving more than $20 for a hanger showing more than the usual wear.

Large (8″) version of Mammy and chef salt and pepper shakers. This set was made in many different color combinations and in all sizes. *Courtesy of Malinda Saunders; photo by Donald Vogt.*

Black boy with umbrella is a potholder hanger. Not shown is a matching girl, facing in the opposite direction, also with an umbrella over her shoulder. *Courtesy of Dakota Sands; photo by Donald Vogt.*

Pair of hanging chalkware plaques, boy and girl with umbrellas, made to be used as kitchen decoration. *Photo by Donald Vogt.*

Salt and pepper shakers of boy and girl eating watermelon. Unmarked. *Courtesy of Dakota Sands; photo by Donald Vogt.*

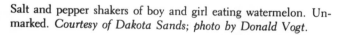

91

Appliquéd and embroidered dish towel shows Mammy flipping pancakes, 1930–1940. With cotton background and multicolored appliquéd pieces, the towel is mostly hand-stitched but parts have been machine-stitched. *Courtesy of Rose Fontanella; photo by Donald Vogt.*

A colorful dish towel has black children dancing all around its border. *Courtesy of Rose Fontanella; photo by Donald Vogt.*

SALT AND PEPPERS

Salt holders originated in medieval times and came to be made in a number of elaborate designs and materials. Pewter, gold, china, and crystal salts are available for the collector.

Salt and pepper sets were introduced during the late nineteenth century and were produced in a wide variety of shapes and sizes and often given away as tourist mementos.

The most common black salt and pepper shakers are in the form of a Mammy and a chef, and can be found in many sizes and colors.

TABLECLOTHS AND DISH TOWELS

Colorfully made out of cotton or linen, towels and tablecloths usually came in sets and were sold throughout the 1930s–1950s. If you are lucky, you may find a tag denoting the manufacturer, but it is not necessary.

With time and repeated washings and use, the pieces become faded and frayed. It is recommended that you stay away from tablecloths with holes, heavily worn spots, or frayed edges. Towels may be more faded than their tablecloth "sisters" so we may allow a little more room for damage; however, one still must draw the line where rips and worn spots are concerned and wait for a better buy sometime in your collecting future.

Most sets were made in three or four different color combinations, so you may find one pattern in red, purple, blue, and yellow versions. The tablecloths are easier to find than the dish towels because they were used less frequently, therefore managing to stay out of the trash.

TOASTER-COVER DOLLS

These "kitchen dolls" were more thoroughly covered in Chapter 5, "Dolls."

Throughout the 1930s, 1940s, and 1950s, toaster dolls were made commercially as well as by hand and were used in the kitchen to cover unsightly appliances such as the toaster and mixer. One can find them in any color combination and each seems to have a personality all its own.

Nowadays collectors use the dolls for their original purpose as well as in the bathroom to cover toilet paper rolls, in the bedroom as pillow accents, and as decorative pieces in a country parlor.

The price you pay for a toaster doll should depend on its age and condition. Because of the recent rise of interest in black Americana, these dolls are not as inexpensive as they were a few years ago and some of the older ones have been seen priced as high as $75.

A sprightly group of toaster dolls, no two exactly alike. *Courtesy of Rose Fontanella; photo by Donald Vogt.*

COMPANIES THAT PRODUCED KITCHEN COLLECTIBLES

F & F Tool and Die Company. Aunt Jemima and Uncle Mose items were sold or given away in advertising promotions for Quaker Oats. Items marked "F & F Tool and Die Co., Dayton, Ohio," were made during the period of 1949–1951 only. This makes those particular objects in the line more desirable and slightly higher priced.

Also made by the F & F Tool and Die Company were the Luzianne Coffee advertising pieces. The Luzianne Mammy is very recognizable, available in salt and pepper shakers of all sizes, and has been seen in two or three different color combinations.

Reproductions are currently on the market and can be recognized easily because the original Luziannes have a green skirt and the repros don't.

McCoy Pottery was founded by James McCoy in 1899. The company has undergone many name changes during its time in business. In 1899, the company name was J. W. McCoy Pottery. In 1903, the firm was rebuilt and in 1909, George S. Brush took over as manager. In 1911, the firm's name became the Brush McCoy pottery company and that name was shortened to the Brush Pottery Company in 1925. In 1933, the company became the Nelson McCoy Pottery Company. McCoy pottery, a division of D. T. Chase Enterprises of Hartford, Connecticut, is still in business. McCoy produced many black cookie jars.

Red Wing Potteries, Inc. began in 1936 in Red Wing, Minnesota, and closed its doors in 1967. The firm is responsible for making vases and planters. However, the Mammy clock is reputed to have been made by the Red Wing firm. They also made several cookie jars during the 1950s.

Shawnee Pottery started in 1937 in Zanesville, Ohio. An executive of the Hull Pottery Company was the original founder of Shawnee. They sold most of their pieces, dinnerware sets as well as kitchen items, to Sears, Roebuck and Company. The pottery went out of business in 1961.

Weller Pottery was founded in 1895 in Zanesville, Ohio, and continued in existence until 1948.

Although Weller's main interest was in vases, wall pockets, and art pottery, they did put out a kitchen set depicting the Aunt Jemima figure. The set is extremely rare and valuable when found today (see above, "Cookie Jars").

PRICE GUIDE—
KITCHEN COLLECTIBLES

DESCRIPTION	APPROXIMATE PRICE
Aunt Jemima, miniature, iron, some wear	$85–$100
Bottle opener, black face, brass	$45–$60
Bottle opener, black man's head, open mouth, wall mounted	$30–$45
Bottle opener, black waiter, holding three steins, wood, 1900s, original paint	$85–$105
Broom dolls, pair, contemporary	$36–$40 each
"Butler" brushes, one green-and-yellow, one black-and-white	$20–$28 each
Candy container, Amos 'n Andy	$375–$400
Chalkware plaques, pair, black boy and girl with umbrellas	$22–$30
Condiment set, Aunt Jemima, spices, salt and pepper, syrup, 11-piece	$160–$175
Cookie jar, Aunt Jemima, celluloid	$60–$110
Cookie jar, Aunt Jemima, ceramic	$45–$65
Cookie jar, black man, McCoy Pottery	$15–$40
Cookie jar, chef, Pearl China	$75–$95
Cookie jar, lady, ceramic	$45–$70
Cookie jar, Mammy, bisque	$20–$30
Cookie jar, Mammy, porcelain	$35–$55
Cookie jar, Mammy with cauliflowers, McCoy Pottery	$275–$375
Creamer, Uncle Mose	$28–$35
Cruet, oil and vinegar, Mammy and chef	$35–$45
Cup and saucer, Coon Chicken Inn, with stand	$65–$80
Dinner bell, Aunt Jemima	$40–$60
Dishcloths, different designs, set of five, ca. 1925	$75–$85
Grocery list, hanging, Aunt Jemima, "I'se Gotta Get," wood	$28–$35
Mammy, sweeping, Lindstrom, boxed	$125–$175
Match holder, Art Deco, waiter	$350–$400
Match holder, wall, with potholder, Aunt Jemima	$35–$45
Pad holder, Mammy Memo	$15–$25
Paper towel holder, Aunt Jemima, wood	$48–$65
Pie bird, black chef	$25–$35
Pie bird, Mammy	$24–$30
Plaque, cook and chef	$40–$60
Potholder, figural, girl	$12–$15
Potholder, wall, chalkware, yellow-and-black Sambo	$25–$40
Rack, potholder, Aunt Jemima, carved, wood	$15–$30
Recipe box, Mammy	$18–$24
Salt and pepper, Aunt Jemima	$12–$20
Salt and pepper, chefs, ceramic, 5″	$10–$15
Salt and pepper, Luzianne, original green skirt	$22–$40
Salt and pepper, Mammy and chef, 4½″	$14–$20
Salt and pepper, Salty and Peppy, Pearl China, 4½″	$25–$35
Shaker, paprika, Aunt Jemima, 4″	$10–$18
Shopping list, on board, holes mark various items, Mammy face at top	$25–$35
Spice set, Luzianne Coffee pieces, six 3″ pieces, salt and pepper 5″ tall	$32–$45
Spice set, Mammy, 6-piece	$75–$85
String holder, Aunt Jemima, wall, porcelain, 6¾″	$12–$15
String holder, Mammy	$30–$40
Sugar and creamer, Aunt Jemima, covered, celluloid	$22–$28
Sugar and creamer, Luzianne Coffee figures, no lids	$62–$68
Sweeper, bread crumb, Mammy, ceramic	$28–$32
Syrup, Aunt Jemima	$15–$20
Tablecloth, linen, 52″ square, 1940s, shows activities of a Southern plantation in red, green, yellow, purple, and black	$75–$85
Tea towel set	$10–$15
Thermometer, Diaper Dan, boxed, 1949, 5″	$85–$95
Tin, Aunt Dinah, 4½″	$20–$25
Toaster doll, blue-and-white dress, button eyes, hand-sewn features	$32–$40
Toaster doll, rubber face, yellow dress and bonnet	$26–$30
Tobacco jar, figural, black boy, 5½″	$85–$95
Tobacco jar, figural, black girl, 5½″	$85–$95
Toothpick holder, Mammy, bisque, 3″	$2–$4
Towel, Aunt Jemima	$20–$30
Towel, kitchen, black chef with lobster	$20–$30
Trivet, Aunt Jemima	$8–$10
Whisk broom, Aunt Jemima	$24–$35

"Butler" brushes, one green-and-yellow, the other black-and-white. *Photo by Donald Vogt.*

Blue-and-white toaster doll has button eyes, hand-sewn features. *Courtesy of Malinda Saunders; photo by Donald Vogt.*

Mammy clock, reputed to have been made by Red Wing Pottery in the 1940s. *Courtesy of Judy Posner; photo by Donald Vogt.*

A pair of contemporary broom dolls. *Courtesy of Jeanie Ohle; photo by Donald Vogt.*

Wooden potholder in the shape of a Mammy, 1940s. *Courtesy of Rose Fontanella; photo by Donald Vogt.*

"Cook's Delight," Mammy and chef spoon rest. *Courtesy of Judy Posner; photo by Donald Vogt.*

Mammy string holder hangs on the wall. Made of composition, she wears a gray dress and apron and has a yellow scarf around her head. *Courtesy of Judy Posner; photo by Donald Vogt.*

White metal bust of Johnny "the boy with the torn hat" Griffin playing banjo, approximately 5″ tall. *Courtesy of Jim Boll-man, The Music Emporium; photo by Donald Vogt.*

11
Music and Theater

Of all the categories in collecting black Americana, music is one of the most interesting and far-reaching. Music transcends time and place, and black people have made a definite, lasting impression on American music.

As a collector you can pick a period of time and concentrate your energies on learning everything there is to know of the black music of that era. You can collect sheet music, instruments, books, figurines, photographs, autographs, paintings, or records. The field is seemingly unending.

Beginning with slave music, my research took me through spirituals, the blues, and the birth of jazz. Each area deserves a chapter in itself, but there isn't the space in a book of this sort to cover all that black music entails.

I have included biographies of music luminaries and information about blackface minstrels. There are many more biographies that could be included in this category, but I wanted to give you, the reader, as much of an overview as possible.

Some may say that I should not have included minstrels in this book because they were not black—but read on. Blackface minstrels were not only white; some were black people as well. And the minstrel era, with all its racial overtones, made a great impact on the musical society of its day.

Hopefully I have given you enough information to at least start you in your musical collecting and to show you the many different avenues you can take.

This chapter could not have been completed without the insight and cooperation of Jim Bollman of The Music Emporium in Cambridge, Massachusetts. Through his extensive knowledge of the subject I learned much about the black musician, the banjo, and the many aspects of early black music. The photographs in this book credited to him show only a small portion of his large and varied collection. I should like to dedicate this chapter to him.

AFRO-AMERICAN MUSIC

Afro-American music began with folk music, whose roots are recognizable in the slave experience and are also associated with work, social activity, and the church. Jazz, the second most important contribution of the Afro-American, was the music of the cabaret and vaudeville house.

Slave Songs of the United States (1867) is the oldest collection of black American songs and serves as the foundation of the study of black American music. The white Northern editors who produced the book were attracted to the beauty of the music, but did not understand its origins or the conditions that produced it. Consequently, the editors did not grasp the music's extraordinary overtones, topical references, and double meanings, as the following examples illustrate.

- The song "Blue Tail Fly," also known as "Jimmy Crack Corn," probably originated with blackface minstrels, but was taken up by slaves. It tells of the slave's delight should his master suffer an untimely death.
- "All the Pretty Horses," an authentic slave lullaby, reveals the bitter feelings of Negro mothers who had to watch over white children and neglect their own.
- During the Underground Railroad days, songs such as "Go Down, Moses" showed the Negro's feeling of persecution. The song is said to be about Harriet Tubman who, as one of the "conductors" of the Railroad, was nicknamed Moses.
- "Steal Away" was sung at many Negro meetings as a signal to those slaves who were to begin their dangerous journey northward.
- "Follow the Drinking Gourd" was a song about the Big Dipper, the stars that pointed north and to freedom.

After working so hard all day, slaves had to release their tensions and often did so by singing and dancing whenever they could. It was reported that the Middlesex Inn near Darien, Connecticut, had a heavy hardwood floor in one room of the house that was "now thin in places from the movement of the merry dancers." The room had been used by slaves for their neighborhood dance.

SPIRITUALS

The spiritual makes use of scriptural fragments and religious ideas. It was popular after 1865 with Christians who felt a deep attachment to God. It is often thought that spirituals were not as popular with the slaves in the eighteenth century as with collectors in the nineteenth century because the slaves had other music that was more expressive of their lot. One possible reason that spirituals gained popularity was the slaves' fear of punishment by white masters. Spirituals did not represent a threat to the masters as did, say, work songs.

Negro spirituals grew out of the fact that the black Americans who sang them were trying to express their sadness and emotional upheaval at having to leave their homelands and learn a new culture, language, and way of life. Titles of the spirituals often show the underlying messages in the songs. "We'll Soon Be Free" sings of jailed Negros. Songs speaking of religion gave the working slave the only solace he knew. One can gauge the misery of the slave and the oppression he felt by tracing the mood of the song.

The Jubilee Singers (1874) was a collection of sixty-one songs, the first collection to contain spirituals exclusively. The majority of the songs are sorrowful—"Nobody Knows the Trouble I See, Lord," "From Every Graveyard," "I'm a Rolling Thro' an Unfriendly World," "We'll Die in the Field," "I'm a Trav'ling to the Grave."

According to *Papers of the Hymn Society of America*, spirituals may be classified into three groups: the call-and-response chant, the slow, lone-phrase melody, and the syncopated, segmented melody. Almost all old spirituals can be fitted into one of these categories.

The spirituals that are sung on stage today by trained choirs lack much of their original sound. The spirituals' true sound does not show predetermined harmony that adheres to music-theory rules.

WORK SONGS

The black man turned to work songs for companionship and as a way to ease the boring repetition and back-breaking effort of his labors. This type of song was recognized and documented as unique in the post–Civil War years.

The songs often deal with the slave's mean white boss or with topics familiar to all the workmen, such as living conditions, people in the community, and pretty women. Often the songs would give a rhythm to the black man's work of laying ties on the railroad, digging ditches, or carrying bales of cotton. The leader would pace the song accordingly until the job was done.

Work songs were primarily men's songs. Women working in the kitchens sang hymns or blues.

MINSTRELS

The first minstrels were white performers who "corked" their faces to travel in blackface minstrel shows.

An Englishman visiting America in 1822 was the first person to introduce Negro stage characters. Charles Matthews studied the dialect, character, history, and actions as well as the songs and lore of black American life. During one of his acts, he used a song called "Possum up a Gum Tree," which is thought to have been the beginning of blackface minstrel shows.

Minstrel shows continued through the early 1800s with such performers as Thomas D. Rice, George Washington Smith, and J. W. Sweeney, who used Negro songs and dances in their routines.

Sheet music from the mid-1800s entitled *Alabama Joe. Courtesy of Jim Bollman, The Music Emporium; photo by Donald Vogt.*

When Harriet Beecher Stowe's *Uncle Tom's Cabin* came to the stage, the comical minstrel characterization of black Americans all but disappeared. Still, the Negro characters were played by whites corking their faces. It was not until the late 1800s that traveling acting troupes began to advertise the inclusion of "real Negro" actors.

Between 1850 and 1910, Negro minstrels such as Thomas Greene Bethume ("Blind Tom"), the Luca family, Horace Weston, and the Hyer sisters performed on the American stage and some even went on to head troupes that traveled all over the world.

By the 1920s, the Negro minstrel shows began to take a back seat to the up-and-coming institution of vaudeville.

BLUES

Songs were also used as entertainment by black people during the development of their own community following the Civil War. Dancing, playing instruments, and celebrating holidays and feast days were newly appreciated in that postwar period.

Music was made on anything that would keep a rhythm. Bones, boxes, saws, pipes, jugs—all were used to make the music to sing the nights away. Social songs of love, gambling, fun, and play developed, and it is thought that this was the period when the "blues" were born.

The Harlem Renaissance in the 1920s gave Negroes a place uniquely theirs in the history of American music. Duke Ellington, Eubie Blake, Noble Sissle, Paul Robeson, Charles Gilpin, Josephine Baker, and Florence Mills made their names on stage and in music.

By the 1930s, the social songs were replaced by the growing popularity of blues and jazz. Blues had its roots, as we have already noted, in early slave laments. They are songs of the individual and of slavery and postslavery experiences. The blues song was a solo song and has remained so.

The text is important to the music and the usual pattern is to repeat the first line, follow with an antecedent phrase, then add a third line.

The blues is rural music, developed in the levees and deltas of the Mississippi, then extending, through riverine connections, throughout the Southwest.

GOSPEL MUSIC

Gospel music is, in a sense, the spiritual of the twentieth century. It is a music that achieves its effects through the singing and its beat. Sometimes it sounds like the blues, sometimes like rock, sometimes like jazz.

Thomas A. Dorsey is thought to have been one of the primary forces in gospel music.

The main difference between spiritual and gospel music is that gospel music is accompanied by the piano and/or other instruments.

JAZZ

Jazz, despite all the fabrications, half-truths, and general misconceptions about it, is basically black music. It is the black man who gave jazz its language, syntax, heart, and vocabulary. It springs from African rhythms and European harmonies and has its roots in the social, racial, economic, and cultural conditions of the South.

New Orleans is famous as the nursery of jazz and is thought to be so because of its reputation as the most liberal Southern city. By 1900 New Orleans was the black musical center of the South.

Although jazz expresses happiness, love of life, and ebullience, it remains protest music.

By the turn of the century, jazz was being represented by brass and marching bands who "ragged" music rhythmically and improvised their tunes. The Creole Jazz Band, led by King Oliver, is perhaps the best-known group from the first period of jazz. Louis Armstrong, a King Oliver sideman, is the best-known single player.

RAGTIME

Ragtime, the music of the first twenty years of the twentieth century, was essentially piano music played hard, brightly, cheerfully, and in a machinelike way. Scott Joplin, James

Ragtime pianist Eubie Blake. *Photo courtesy of Mildred Franklin.*

Large (2' × 3') full-color poster on cardboard for J. C. Rockwell's Big City Show "The Sunny South," one of the first musicals to feature "all colored people." *Courtesy of Rose Fontanella; photo by Donald Vogt.*

Sheet music featuring the works of ten-year-old pianist "Blind Tom." *Courtesy of Valerie Bertrand Collection; photo by Donald Vogt.*

Scott, Artie Matthews, and Louis Chauvin were among the most important black American ragtime musicians.

SHEET MUSIC

Music was decorated as early as the fifteenth century when monks hand-lettered songs for the church. Sheet music that is considered collectible today consists of pieces issued from 1820 on.

The introduction of a better way to print the covers of sheet music not only made them more attractive, but added to the salability of the music. Between 1820 and 1900, an estimated 100,000 different music covers are said to have been sold in the United States. It was an accepted social accomplishment in the Victorian era to sing, read music, and play a musical instrument—thus adding to the popularity of sheet music.

By the mid-nineteenth century, sheet music had reached its peak and by 1870, standards had deteriorated. By the outbreak of World War I, the covers were poorly drawn and garishly decorated.

Age can usually be discerned by the size of the picture on the cover. If it is small, chances are the sheet music is old.

A chalk-and-oil crayon sketch by a Polish artist, dated 1929 and signed in the lower right-hand corner "L. de Mar-kiewicz," shows an American jazz band that traveled to Europe in the 1920s and 1930s. *Courtesy of Ann and Martin Ellman; photo by Donald Vogt.*

"Nodder" from the 1930s depicts Louis Armstrong. *Courtesy of Jim Bollman, The Music Emporium; photo by Donald Vogt.*

Larger pictures with the title in decorative type came into fashion around 1870, and color was added as early as 1840. Chromolithographs were first used in 1843.

Music sheets of the nineteenth and early twentieth centuries are a valuable source of information on the fads, historical events, and feelings of the people of the day. Music sheets announced the first all-professional baseball team, the Adams Express Company's continent-spanning services, the tragic Johnstown flood, the popularity of the high-wheeled bike, and the prejudice toward "men of color."

Some of the best covers were made before the 1930s. Especially collectible are pieces of sheet music illustrated by Currier and Ives, Louis Prang, Winslow Homer, and Sarony. Other desirable artists include James Montgomery Flagg, Pfeiffer, Wholman, Archie Gunn, Norman Rockwell, and Frederick S. Manning.

The value of sheet music is determined by age, condition, rarity, artist, and category.

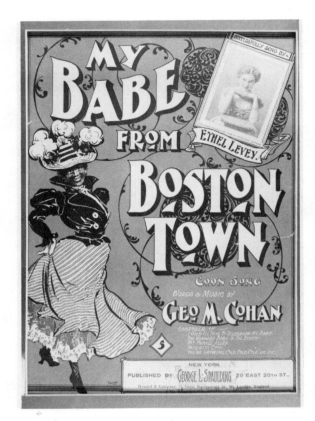

My Babe from Boston Town, words and music by George M. Cohan, labeled on cover a "coon song." *Courtesy of Gwendolyn Goldman; photo by Donald Vogt.*

Turn-of-the-century sheet music entitled *Uncle Jasper's Jubilee.* *Collection of Joseph W. and Nathan Wood; photo by Donald Vogt.*

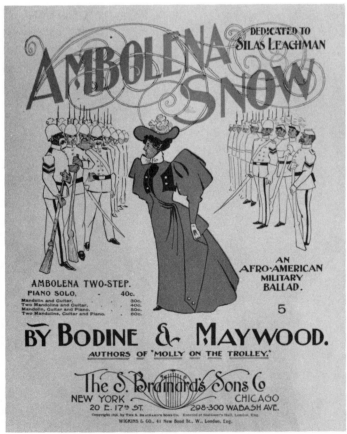

Sheet music entitled *Ambolena Snow,* an Afro-American military ballad. *Courtesy of Valerie Bertrand Collection; photo by Donald Vogt.*

SOME MUSIC/THEATER PERSONALITIES

Amos 'n Andy started out as a vaudeville team named Sam 'n Henry. When they were put on nationwide radio, they changed their name to Amos 'n Andy. Their radio show was successful from 1926 to 1956, at which time they became a hit CBS TV show.

In 1930 they starred in their own movie, *Check and Double Check*, but audiences were disappointed to see their favorite radio characters on screen in blackface.

Many articles have been made that show the Amos 'n Andy images. See Chapter 13, "Toys," for more information.

Louis Armstrong (1900–1971), a New Orleans native, has been called the greatest jazz trumpet player in music history.

As a child he followed jazz bands around the streets of New Orleans and played his trumpet on Mississippi riverboats and in marching bands. In 1922 Joe "King" Oliver asked Armstrong to play second trumpet in his Chicago-based band. Armstrong made a series of records with Oliver's Creole Jazz Band, including *Canal Street Blues*.

Armstrong broke the convention of three-instrument lines in jazz bands by introducing the solo jazz trumpet. He also introduced "scat" singing to millions of listeners who would not usually have listened to jazz. (Scat is a vocal in which meaningless syllables substitute for words.)

Armstrong was a band leader, singer, musician, film star, and comedian. He was also a composer, writing such songs as "I wish I could shimmy like my sister Kate" (with Clarence Williams), "Wild Man Blues" (with Jelly Roll Morton), "Gut Bucket Blues," and many others.

Josephine Baker, born in St. Louis, Missouri, on June 3, 1906, was a famous French stage personality and naturalized French citizen when she died in Paris on April 12, 1975.

Baker was at the head of the wave of interest in Afro-American culture that swept Paris in the 1920s. Her extravagant gestures and bold ·deeds—such as walking her pet leopard down the Champs-Élysées—were part of her flamboyant personality.

She was touring Philadelphia with a dance troupe at sixteen and at seventeen had joined the chorus of a Boston show. Baker advanced steadily until she became part of the floor show of the Plantation Club in Harlem.

Paris beckoned in 1925 and she crossed the ocean to dance in La Revue Nègre and at the Théâtre des Champs-Élysées. She became naturalized in 1937.

Although she starred in a light opera and made several films before World War II, Baker devoted herself to working with the Red Cross and the Resistance during the war. As a result of her actions, she was awarded the Croix de Guerre and the Legion of Honor with the rosette of the Resistance.

After World War II her estate in southwestern France, Les Milandes, took most of her attention. In the 1950s she began adopting babies of all nationalities to fulfill a desire to have what she called "a rainbow family."

She retired from the stage in 1956 but starred in *Paris* in 1959 because she needed money to maintain Les Milandes. In 1949 her *Memoires* were published.

Baker was active in Civil Rights demonstrations in the United States during the 1960s and made her return to the New York stage in 1973.

Charles "Buddy" Bolden was one of the black musicians who originated jazz in the Storyville section of New Orleans in the late 1800s. He organized the first jazz band in 1897 and won the title "King" by popular acclaim.

Harry Thacker Burleigh was born in Erie, Pennsylvania, on December 2, 1866, and died in Stamford, Connecticut, on September 12, 1949. He was known as a baritone and as a composer who transcribed Negro spirituals. After studying under Antonin Dvořák at the National Conservatory of Music in New York City, he taught Dvořák American Negro music.

Burleigh composed more than 200 songs and became known for his arrangements of Negro spirituals. In 1916 he won the Spingarn Medal for the highest achievement by an American Negro. He sang for King Edward VII of England on two occasions and at J. P. Morgan's home as well as at his funeral.

Duke Ellington (real name Edward Kennedy Ellington, 1899–1974), one of the most eminent jazz musicians of the twentieth century, was a composer, pianist, and jazz orchestra leader. As a child he studied piano and at seventeen began to play professionally. Though his parents had oriented him to the fine arts, he chose to play jazz.

He developed his "jungle style" through his band which consisted of musicians such as Bubber Miley and Tricky Sam Nanton. Ellington led a band from 1927 to 1932 at Harlem's Cotton Club and during that period developed a purely Ellingtonian style.

Although "Mood Indigo" brought him widespread fame, pieces played during the late 1930s also attracted world attention. "Bojangles" and "Blue Serge" were two of the other songs Ellington and his band made popular.

During the 1940s Ellington composed concerts and appeared at Carnegie Hall in New York City. The band made world tours in the 1950s, during which period Ellington was also composing motion-picture soundtracks for such movies as *Anatomy of a Murder*, directed by Otto Preminger.

Ellington is also known for "religious jazz." His *In the Beginning God* was performed at St. Michael's Cathedral in England, in New York City, and at West German churches in 1966. *Music Is My Mistress*, his autobiography, was published in 1974.

Lt. J. R. Europe and his Regimental Band are credited with introducing jazz to the French.

Newport Gardner was the slave of Caleb Gardner of Newport, Rhode Island. He was given music lessons while a slave and was found to excel as a teacher. He opened a music school in Newport where he taught both black and white students. In 1791 he won $2,000 in a lottery and bought freedom for himself and his family.

Johann Christian Gotlieb Graupner became known as the "Father of Negro Songs." He sang "The Gay Negro Boy" and accompanied himself on the banjo on December 30, 1799, at the Federal Street Theatre in Boston, Massachusetts.

Elizabeth Taylor Greenfield (1809–1876) was nicknamed "the Black Swan." She was a nineteenth-century soprano whose singing was world acclaimed.

William Christopher Handy (1873–1958) was a composer whose best-known work is the classic "St. Louis Blues." His father and grandfather were ministers but Handy, after graduation from Teachers Agricultural and Mechanical College in Huntsville, Alabama, broke family tradition to work as a bandmaster and schoolteacher.

From 1903 to 1921 he conducted his own orchestra, even though he was struck blind at the age of thirty.

Handy was one of the musicians who worked through the ragtime-to-jazz transition period. As with other black musicians of the day, Handy drew on Negro folklore melodies and added harmonizations to those tunes when working out his orchestral arrangements.

Handy introduced the element of blues into the popular ragtime and wrote such songs as "Memphis Blues," a campaign song for Mayor Edward "Boss" Crump of Memphis in 1911, and the popular "St. Louis Blues" in 1914.

Because he was forced to publish "St. Louis Blues" on his own, Handy formed his own publishing company and directed it until late in life. His firm published studies of U.S. black musicians as well as anthologies of Negro spirituals and blues.

Handy's autobiography, *Father of the Blues*, was published in 1941.

Lorraine Hansberry (1930–1965), author of the play *A Raisin in the Sun*, was the first black playwright to win the New York Drama Critics Award, for the best play of 1959.

Billie Holiday (real name Eleanora Gough McKay) was born in Baltimore on April 7, 1915, and died in New York City on July 17, 1959. Her father, an itinerant guitarist, exposed her to her first jazz recordings. He also introduced her to the world of musicians and their behind-the-scenes activities.

Holiday was a prostitute for a while before making her singing debut in 1931 at a Harlem nightclub. She recorded her first album two years later. In 1935 she was finally recognized as a jazz singer and for a few years after that she toured with such bands as Count Basie's and Artie Shaw's. Although she broke from them in 1940 to become a solo nightclub act, she never severed her affiliations with jazz bands.

Holiday was considered a memorable jazz talent though she entered the music scene with no technical knowledge. Her voice and diction remained superb even throughout her later years when her heroin addiction overtook her. Music critics believed her best years to be 1936–1943, when she recorded with saxophonist Lester Young.

Lady Sings the Blues, her autobiography, was published in 1956. The movie of the same name starred another great singer, Diana Ross, in 1972.

Mahalia Jackson was born on October 26, 1911, in New Orleans and became a great gospel singer whose religion was an intense part of her life.

She sang at the age of five in her father's choir and became familiar with singers such as Bessie Smith. Jackson went to Chicago at the age of sixteen and began singing in Baptist churches. A wise and prudent woman, she invested her earnings in real estate.

After 1945, her fame spread throughout the United States and her recordings of "Move On Up a Little Higher" and "Silent Night" were very successful. Jackson's music undeniably proved that a link exists between religious music and jazz.

James Weldon Johnson was born in Jacksonville, Florida, on June 17, 1871, and died in Wiscasset, Maine, on June 26, 1938. He was well known as a poet, a diplomat, and an anthologist as well as an accomplished musician.

His schoolteacher mother trained him in music as a boy and helped him gain a B.A. from Atlanta University in 1894. He also received an M.A. from Atlanta in 1904 and later studied at Columbia University. He became the principal of a Jacksonville, Florida, high school, a lawyer—admitted to the Florida bar in 1897—and a composer.

With his brother, John, Johnson wrote the Negro national anthem "Lift Every Voice and Sing" and together the brothers wrote more than 200 songs for the musical stage.

In 1906 President Theodore Roosevelt appointed Johnson as U.S. consul in Puerto Cabello, Venezuela. He was given other diplomatic assignments after that time and served until 1914.

In 1912 his novel, *Autobiography of an Ex-Coloured Man*, was published anonymously. In 1927, the book was reissued under his name and got a better reception than it had its first time out.

He was connected with the NAACP, serving as executive secretary of that organization until 1930. His poetry is well known and admired and his discussions of Negro jazz, folk music, and theater are considered some of the most perceptive statements ever made.

The Jubilee Singers from Fisk University introduced Negro spirituals to the musical world in 1871. Included in their large repertoire were such songs as "Steal Away to Jesus," "Freedom Over Me," "Nobody Knows the Trouble I See," and "Swing Low, Sweet Chariot."

Hattie McDaniel (1898–1952) was a radio and film actress. She was the first black female to win the Academy Award for her supporting role in *Gone With the Wind* in 1939. She also played Beulah in the television series of the same name.

Sidney Poitier, the well-known film star, was the first black actor to record his footprints in Grauman's Chinese Theater in Los Angeles, California, in 1967.

Florence B. Price (1888–1953) was the first black woman composer to achieve national recognition. She won the Wanamaker Foundation Award for her Symphony in E Minor in 1925.

Paul Robeson, born in 1898, was the son of a former slave

The singer Josephine Baker. *From the collection of Mildred Franklin.*

Autographed photograph of W. C. Handy, musician known for popularizing the blues, who died in 1958. *Courtesy of the Valerie Bertrand Collection; photo by Donald Vogt.*

but overcame that stigma to become a singer, actor, All-American football player, and black activist.

Educated at Rutgers University and its star football player, Robeson was also at the head of his class. In 1923 he received a law degree, but because of a lack of opportunity in that field, became a stage performer in London.

Eugene O'Neill's play *Emperor Jones* made Robeson known worldwide. The play caused a sensation in 1924 in New York, was taken to London in 1925 and made into a film in 1933. Robeson was also well known for his part as Joe in *Show Boat*. His version of "Ol' Man River" was often the highlighted performance of the show. Robeson also performed Shakespeare in London and on Broadway.

In 1934 Robeson visited the Soviet Union and developed left-wing commitments. The United States withdrew his passport in 1950 because of his failure to sign a disclaimer denying membership in the Communist party. Although the Supreme Court later overturned the ruling (in 1958), Robeson was ostracized from that time on because of his political views.

He died in Philadelphia on January 23, 1976.

Bessie Smith was also born in 1898. She grew up in a poor family in Tennessee but became one of the greatest female blues singers of the early twentieth century.

She was inspired and helped by "Ma" Rainey, the first of the great blues singers. During the early part of her career, Smith traveled through the smaller theaters of the Southern states, learning her craft. Clarence Williams, a representative of Columbia Records, discovered Smith and helped her record her first record in February 1923.

Although Smith was known during the 1920s as "the Empress of the Blues," the style of music changed and she was no longer at the top of the mountain. She became an alcoholic and lost control of her career.

Smith made well over 150 recordings and starred in the movie *St. Louis Blues* in 1929. The movie, banned then, is now preserved in the Museum of Modern Art in New York City.

She died on September 26, 1937, in Clarksdale, Mississippi, as a result of injuries sustained in an automobile accident.

PRICE GUIDE—MUSICAL ITEMS

DESCRIPTION	APPROXIMATE PRICE

Book, John Tasker Howard, *Our American Music: Three Hundred Years of It,* 1931, New York .... $10–$15

Book, Langston Hughes, *The First Book of Jazz,* 1955, New York .... $15–$20

Book, James W. Johnson, editor, *The Second Book of Negro Spirituals,* 1926, New York .... $10–$15

Book, Francis Lewidge, *Songs of the Fields,* 1916, New York ....$7–$10

Book, J. B. T. Marsh, *The Story of the Jubilee Singers; With Their Songs,* 1881, Boston ...... $15–$20

Bookends, carved wood, singing man with guitar .. $35–$40

Figurine, black drummer .... $25–$35

Figurine, Negro musicians, bisque, 5-piece....... $120–$150

Hotel menu, signed by Duke Ellington, ca. 1940 .... $10–$12

Photographs, Chuck Berry, three signed, one in purple ink .... $25–$30

Photographs, Fats Domino, seated at piano, 8″ × 10″ signed .... $4–$6

Photograph, Duke Ellington, signed .... $20–$25

Poster, "The Parade of the Darktown Wangdoodles" .... $30–$50

Poster, "You'se Worn Dat Face Too Long," ca. 1898 .... $30–$50

Record, Louis Armstrong, 1926........................ $50–$55

Record, Nat King Cole, *Forgive My Heart* .... $20–$25

Record, Fats Domino, *Counting Boy and If You Need Me* .... $2–$5

Record, Duke Ellington with his orchestra, *Creole Love Call,* Victor, c. 1927 .... $12–$18

Record, Duke Ellington with the Jungle Band, *Mood Indigo,* Brunswick, c. 1930 .... $12–$18

Record, Duke Ellington with his orchestra, *Rockabye River,* Victor, ca. 1946 .... $4–$8

Records, collection of 36 original phonograph, along with 16 signed photos and other items, in leather-bound albums .... $400–$425

Sheet music, "Ah wants to die from eatin' possum pie," 1922 .... $6–$8

Sheet music, "A Little Bit o' Honey," oval of mother and child .... $10–$12

Sheet music, Amos 'n Andy .... $12–$15

Sheet music, Amos 'n Andy, *The Pepsodent Hour*.. $20–$25

Sheet music, "And they called it Dixieland" ...... $25–$35

Sheet music, "Angel Eyes," Nat King Cole........... $5–$7

Sheet music, "The Colored Major," march and two-step .... $30–$35

Sheet music, "Coontown Troubles," 1909 .... $10–$15

Sheet music, "Darktown Strutter's Ball," 1917 .... $15–$20

Sheet music, "Ev'ry Darkey Had a Raglan On," 1901 .... $10–$15

Autographed photograph of Ella Fitzgerald. *Courtesy of Mildred Franklin Collection.*

Sheet music, "Dis Ain't No Time for an Argument," 1906................................... $10–$15

Sheet music, "Mandy Lou," words and music by Thomas S. Allen .... $30–$35

Sheet music, "Moonlight on the Melon Patch" .. $25–$40

Sheet music, "My Babe from Boston Town," words and music by George M. Cohan .... $20–$30

Sheet music, "Old Black Joe," 1906 ....$8–$10

Sheet music, "Shortnin' Bread," black lithograph ...$6–$10

Sheet music, "Uncle Jaspar's Jubilee" .... $100–$175

Sheet music, "Zip-A-Dee-Doo-Dah" .... $12–$20

Violin, mahogany, head of black woman carved on neck .... $1,500–$3,000

Autographed photograph of opera star Leontyne Price. *Courtesy of Mildred Franklin Collection.*

(Below)
A theater program features Billie Holiday starring in a Midnight Variety Concert. *Courtesy of the Valerie Bertrand Collection; photo by Donald Vogt.*

Ernest Anderson presents
FRED ROBBINS'
ONE-NITE STAND
A Midnight Variety Concert
starring

Autographed photograph of Lena Horne. *Courtesy of Mildred Franklin Collection.*

Autographed photograph of Marian Anderson. *Courtesy of Mildred Franklin Collection.*

Autographed photograph of actress Ethel Waters. *Courtesy of Mildred Franklin Collection.*

Autographed photograph of 1940s dancer/entertainer Peg Leg Bates. *Courtesy of the Valerie Bertrand Collection; photo by Donald Vogt.*

The Negro in the American Theatre, by Edith J. R. Isaacs. *Courtesy of the Valerie Bertrand Collection; photo by Donald Vogt.*

Music poster, "The Parade of the Darktown Wangdoodles." *Courtesy of Gwendolyn Goldman; photo by Donald Vogt.*

Ambrotype of blackface banjo player and dancer. *Courtesy of Jim Bollman, The Music Emporium; photo by Donald Vogt.*

Music poster, ca. 1898, "You'se Worn Dat Face Too Long." *Courtesy of Gwendolyn Goldman; photo by Donald Vogt.*

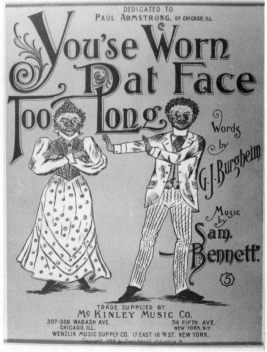

A very pouty baby girl on a very fancy wicker chair. The carte de visite was taken by a photography studio in Texas at the turn of the century and marked on the back, "Miss Bessie Barratt." *Courtesy of Dawn Reno; photo by Donald Vogt.*

12
Photographica

ABOUT PHOTOGRAPHY

Photography was developed over a period of centuries, beginning with Leonardo da Vinci's description of the *camera obscura*. In 1822 Nicephore Niepce, a Frenchman, developed the first fixing agent to produce a permanent photograph. The daguerreotype process was fully developed by 1839, but roll film, developed by George Eastman, did not come into use until 1884 and the first Kodak camera did not come on the market until 1888.

By the 1850s, photography in the United States became a widely practiced craft that rivaled painting. Portraits of famous people were daguerreotypes instead of oil paintings. Photographs were dubbed "portraits for the poor."

Collecting old photographs of black Americans can be a fascinating and time-consuming hobby. Although photographs were often discarded from old frames, there are now enough collectors in the world to make the photographs as viable a part of the antiques world as their gilded frames. Not bad for an area that achieved prominence just fourteen years ago when Sotheby's was the first auction house to devote an auction to the subject of "photographica."

Daguerreotypes and other portraits had been made by black photographers from the earliest days of photography in the United States. When the demand for portraits grew stronger, studios run by black entrepreneurs became commercially successful.

From the beginning, as with the other arts, black photographers faced a tougher road than did their white compatriots. They did not have the money or the free time to indulge in artistic pursuits, nor did they enter other photographic fields, such as photojournalism or advertising, in large numbers until after World War II.

Various black photographers worked after World War II and into the 1960s. Bruce Davidson worked in East Harlem and on subways in New York while Eugene Richards worked in the poor areas of Boston. Roland Freeman chronicled the poor in Baltimore.

During the 1960s, professional black photographers emerged and gave something of themselves to the troubled era. The first *Black Photographer's Annual* appeared in 1973.

THE PHOTOGRAPHERS

Mathew B. Brady (1823–1896) was America's foremost nineteenth-century photographer. His portraits of politicians and views of the Civil War are represented in textbooks all over the world. Brady also photographed every president from John Quincy Adams to William McKinley.

In 1861, when the Civil War broke out, Brady decided to make a complete pictorial record of the war. He hired a staff of twenty photographers and dispatched them throughout the war zones. Brady personally photographed the battles at Bull Run, Antietam, and Gettysburg, as well as Robert E. Lee's surrender at Appomattox. Though not black themselves, he and his staff are responsible for the majority of photographs taken of black Americans during the Civil War period.

In 1873, Brady was forced into bankruptcy and the War Department later bought his plates for $2,840 at public auction. He died alone in a hospital charity ward.

Bruce Davidson, born in 1933, studied at the Rochester Institute of Technology and at Yale. His work is candid; as he describes it, "I look at people with my camera, but as much to find out what's inside me—to reflect my own emotional state, the struggles, the states of consciousness and to discover who the person was who took the picture."

Davidson was a member of the Magnum photo agency since 1958 and did photos for such magazines as *Life*, *Vogue*, and *Esquire*. During the 1970s he began a new interest, filmmaking, and later wrote the screenplay for Isaac Bashevis Singer's *Enemies: A Love Story*. His photo essay "Black Americans" was done during the years 1962–1965.

Collections of Davidson's work are held by the Chicago, Harvard, Kansas, Metropolitan, Modern Art, Nebraska, Smithsonian, and Yale museums.

Robert Scott Duncanson, active during the middle to late 1800s, was listed as a daguerreotype artist in the 1851–1852 *Cincinnati Art Directory*. He often used his camera to capture landscapes, which he would later paint. One of his daguerreotypes, *View of Cincinnati, Ohio, from Covington, Kentucky*, remains one of the few city scenes of life in early nineteenth-century America.

See Chapter 2 for more information on this artist.

Sepia-toned photograph of "Happy John" with his banjo. Photographer's mark in lower right-hand corner. *Courtesy of Jim Bollman, The Music Emporium; photo by Donald Vogt.*

Worn carte de visite of a black cowboy, taken by an Ardmore, Texas, photographer, 1875–1885. *Courtesy of Dawn Reno; photo by Donald Vogt.*

Danny Lyon was born in 1942 and received his B.A. from the University of Chicago in 1963. He joined the Student Non-Violent Coordinating Committee (SNCC) in 1963 and became a photographer who documented the Civil Rights movement. He later used his photographs of that era in *The Movement.*

Lyon is a controversial photographer, with a number of unusual credits, including photographs he took while a motorcycle club member. He has been active in cinema since 1960 and has directed at least four films.

Collections of his work are held by the Houston, International Photography, Modern Art, and New Mexico museums.

Jules Lyon. It is a little-known fact that during the early days of photography's popularity in America, a mulatto artist from Louisiana named Jules Lyon introduced the daguerreotype to the people of New Orleans.

He took photographs of the St. Louis Hotel, the cathedral, the levee, and other public buildings and places, and his daguerreotypes were appreciated as being precise, artistic reproductions of the original objects.

Lyon was born in Paris and was only twenty-six in 1839 when he made his debut in New Orleans. Even at that tender age, he had already exhibited in the Paris Salon (in 1831). Following his desire to make the daguerreotype a new form of art, Lyon studied with Louis Jacques Mande Daguerre in Paris for approximately a year, then came back to New Orleans in 1843 to move to a larger studio. Once again the New Orleans residents praised his work as an artist, lithographer, and photographer.

In 1846 he began a series of political portraits for the *New Orleans Bee*, but was unable to complete the project because the owner of the paper died.

Lyon's best work is said to be his *Portrait of John J. Audubon,* the well-known naturalist and illustrator. Jules Lyon spent the balance of his career between Paris and New Orleans until his death in 1866.

James Van Der Zee was born in 1886 in New York City, where his mother and father worked as Ulysses S. Grant's maid and butler. James was raised in Lenox, Massachusetts. In 1900, he won a camera outfit and embarked on a career in photography.

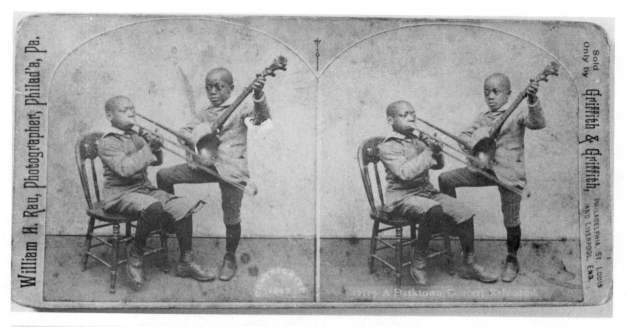

He opened his first studio in Harlem in 1916 and photographed weddings, funerals, and other social occasions in that area for over fifty years.

Van Der Zee was the largest contributor to a photography exhibit called "Harlem on My Mind," held at the Metropolitan Museum of Art in New York in 1969.

Van Der Zee prints are expensive when they can be bought at auction and are currently enjoying a surge in interest. Collections of his work can be seen at the Metropolitan Museum in New York and in museums in New Orleans and San Francisco.

(Top)
Stereoptic view of two youngsters with their musical instruments. Signed by William H. Rau, photographer, Philadelphia. *Courtesy of Jim Bollman, The Music Emporium; photo by Donald Vogt.*

(Above)
Stereoptic view of black boy "A Tunnin' on the Old Banjo," signed by William H. Rau, Photographer, Philadelphia. *Courtesy of Jim Bollman, The Music Emporium; photo by Donald Vogt.*

Sepia-toned photograph of a young woman with her guitar. *Courtesy of Jim Bollman, The Music Emporium; photo by Donald Vogt.*

Members of the White Fawn Country Club with their "entertainers." Sepia-toned photograph, 1900–1910. *Courtesy of Jim Bollman, The Music Emporium; photo by Donald Vogt.*

Civil War photograph of soldiers watching two black men ready their birds for a cockfight. *Courtesy of Lee Galleries; photo by Donald Vogt.*

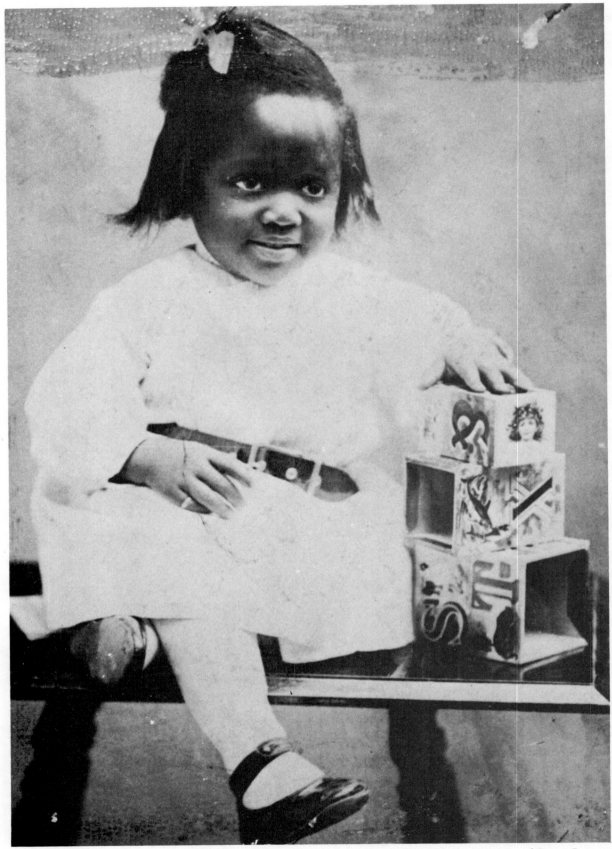

Victorian carte de visite, or photographic calling card, of black girl with building blocks. *Courtesy of Dawn Reno; photo by Donald Vogt.*

PRICE GUIDE—PHOTOGRAPHICA

DESCRIPTION   *APPROXIMATE PRICE*

Ambrotype, black child with white doll, case,
     sixth plate .... $300–$375
Ambrotype, black girl .... $175–$200
Carte de visite, black male dressed in rags,
     patch over left eye, umbrella in left hand,
     fan in right hand .... $32–$40
Carte de visite, boy with Civil War cap,
     ca. 1875 .... $35–$50
Daguerreotype, black baby............................ $115–$150
Daguerreotype case, gutta percha, black man,
     oval .... $55–$75
Daguerreotype case, gutta percha, Victorian
     black girl.. $75–$90
Family album, 600 shots, New London, Conn.,
     family .... $255–$355
Film, *The Life of Booker T. Washington:*
     From Slave Cabin to Hall of Fame.......... $125–$250
Glass plate, picking cotton on Mississippi
     plantation.. $20–$35
Glass slides, three different views of natives, ca.
     1920 .... $28–$35
Imperial carte, New Year's greeting 1891,
     Mammy with baby on lap .... $125–$140
Magic lantern slides, colored, portion of story
     on each one, "The Little Nigger Boys,"
     complete.. $200–$275
Magic lantern slides, two boxers, in dress clothes
     and top hats... $38–$45
Photograph, black and white women making
     baskets, signed Margaret Bourne.............. $325–$400
Photograph, black exercise boy with five horses,
     outside stables .... $35–$50
Photograph of Dinah Washington, framed .... $45–$60
Photograph, NAACP Wartime Conference,
     July 12–14, 1944 .... $175–$225
Photograph, thirteen different sepia views,
     children and adults at work in
     Florida and Georgia............................. $225–$325
Record of marriage of Miles Harris and Nannies Gordon,
     Louisville, Kentucky, December 11, 1873,
     along with ten tintypes and
     one carte de visite .... $58–$75
Stereo card, black boy eating watermelon,
     set of four .... $25–$40
Stereoptic view, "15th Amendment bringing
     his crop to town" .... $18–$28
Stereoptic view, "Golly! Dis am cheaper dan
     twofers" .... $12–$20
Stereoptic view, "Happy Hours," girl picking
     boy's head.. $18–$22
Stereoptic view, old man in cart, pulled by
     oxen .... $25–$35

Stereoptic view, "Six pickers in cotton field,"
     James M. Davis, 1892............................. $15–$20
Tintype, black baby in crib, full plate .... $125–$140
Tintype, black girl child, plaid dress, 3″ × 3½″.... $55–$75
Tintype, black man, 6½″ × 8½″ .... $35–$45
Tintype, Mammy with child identified as Jenny
     Jolly and John Carhart .... $68–$90
Tintype, nurse with two children .... $58–$70
Tintypes, group of fourteen, black people thought
     to be members of Frederick Douglass's family,
     Rochester, New York .... $140–$165

A trio of commercially produced marionettes, made during the 1920s and 1930s. *Courtesy of Rose Fontanella; photo by Donald Vogt.*

13

Toys

If you are lucky enough to afford the luxury of collecting black toys, you have selected a field that spans well over two centuries and includes articles made of an assortment of materials, in diverse ways and manners. And don't be alarmed by my comments about prices; there are still areas of toy collecting that can be invaded with a small pocketbook. The better toys are high in price, but those made in the twentieth century, especially plastic ones, are still reasonable enough for the average American to afford. You must hunt these lesser-priced items down and get them into your collection quickly, however, because toys tend to rise in price the moment a new owner purchases them.

Because you will be collecting items made of tin, cast iron, wood, and paper, the methods for preserving and caring for each will be different and you should take the time to learn each one.

You should also take into consideration how to display such a collection. Since you usually don't have to worry about adjusting the room temperature and since dust will not normally affect tin, cast iron, or wood, the task is a pleasurable one. Just remember that paper toys will not stand the abuse that the others will and special care must be taken to preserve them. Displaying your toys can be one of the most interesting things about collecting them. Who could resist a fireplace mantel full of movable tin toys, a cabinet displaying iron banks, or a bedroom lined with shelves that hold the prettiest of the automatic toys? There's always an interesting way to display the playthings of children. For more ideas, check the magazines that currently tout the collecting craze. They usually have a section devoted to the way various people display their antiques, and many ideas can be adapted or borrowed for your own home.

Toy collectors have always been attracted to toys that depict black characters. Prices have skyrocketed with recent interest shown in the category, and black toys now command an average of $50 to $100, with rare examples reaching into the thousands.

Don't buy a toy you aren't familiar with unless it is cheap enough to allow you the luxury of researching its background later. What you may think is a perfect piece may have one or more essential parts missing and, as we have already learned, that fact will decrease the value of anything that is considered antique or collectible.

Cast-iron toys have been reproduced (as have cast-iron banks) and the buyer should be extremely comfortable with the piece's originality before plunking down a sizable amount of money. Nothing is more heartbreaking than to pay a high price for what you believe to be an antique, only to find out later it is a cheap reproduction.

Most toy dealers and collectors will agree with me when I say that you should buy the best example you can afford. Should you be like most collectors, there will be a day when you want to upgrade your collection by selling off the lower-end items. You will only become frustrated and disappointed if you cannot sell your toys because they are damaged or not all original. They may have seemed like bargains when you bought them, but in the antiques world there are few bargains we don't have to pay for sometime in the future. My husband calls such bad buys "gronks." By his definition, a "gronk" is a thing that excites you momentarily—enough to give your hard-earned money to own it—but grieves you endlessly, because you can't sell it for the amount you paid for it.

Information about specific toys not covered in this chapter—and there will be many because the field is seemingly endless—can be obtained from books on the subject, from toy museums such as the Margaret Woodbury Strong Museum in Rochester, New York, or the Brooklyn Children's Museum in New York City, as well as from the dealers whose speciality is toys. There are also antiques shows that feature just toys and dolls. A small fee will cover your entrance to the show for a day and if you take the time to wander around and ask questions, chances are you will come out much more knowledgeable about black toys than when you went in.

AN INTRODUCTION TO TOYS

Toys are as old as mankind itself and examples have survived from the earliest periods of time. Dolls, glass or pottery beads, figurines made of ivory, silver, or wood, are among the most common early toys.

Toys were first produced commercially in Germany during late medieval times and the superior toy makers of that region began producing such wonders as mechanical toys as early as the nineteenth century. Yet American manufacturers soon caught up with the more experienced Europeans and would

Mechanical toy, boy holding tray. He wears black checked knickers, an orange coat, white shirt with blue dots, a large pink-and-black striped bow tie, and yellow shoes. He also moves his head. *Courtesy of the Shelburne Museum, Shelburne, Vermont.*

eventually bypass them with their more advanced technologies.

Wooden toys were the most popular children's item from the beginning of colonial times until the introduction of tin around 1840. Local carvers made rocking horses, dolls, animals, dollhouses, whirligigs, and mechanical contrivances. Because such toys were not mass-produced and often not signed, and because their makers were, by and large, not professionals, we have gotten into the habit of placing wooden "folky" toys alongside folk art. Many of the early wooden toys were made as gifts for small children, therefore only one of the item was made, classifying it as folk art, to be held much dearer than those items that are far more common.

When tin toys were introduced, they were made by more toy makers in more abundance than wooden toys, which took many hours to complete even if the maker was a skilled craftsman. Tin windup toys that danced a jig or played a musical instrument became the rage. In the 1870s one manufacturer was known to have produced 40 million toys annually.

Tin, cast iron, and plastic were revolutionary materials at the end of the nineteenth century but are now widely used, and new materials are constantly being discovered.

Toys often reflect the times during which they are produced, but old favorites such as dolls, moving vehicles, and rattles seem to be the mainstays of the toy industry.

Toys depicting black people began to appear shortly after the Civil War, with the exception of dolls, which had been made for many years. The majority of black toys appeared during the late 1880s and 1890s.

Although the exaggerated image of the black person as big-lipped and wide-eyed with flared nostrils began in the South, it was the Northern manufacturers who capitalized on that unfavorable image in order to sell products.

It was not until the late 1880s and 1890s that European toy makers began manufacturing black-oriented items. Should you have the chance to compare the American-made toys to the European, you will see a distinct difference. The European-manufactured toys are much more realistic when showing the black face, and the figures tend to be dressed in more fashionable clothes than black Americans would normally have worn.

During the latter part of the nineteenth century, it is interesting to note most toys and games were minstrel-oriented. By the turn of the century and before World War I, blackface and Negro minstrel troupes were traveling throughout Europe and the United States, which may explain why so many toys were made in the minstrels' image. German toy makers, such as the Bing and Lehmann companies, produced hundreds of minstrel-oriented toys.

By that time, American industries were producing toys that had previously been imported from Europe. Tin toys with movable parts, iron banks, both mechanical and still, and riding toys were being made to satisfy the demand for children's playthings. American toys were not only competing with the foreign toy market but were even in demand in Europe and South America.

Parlor games entranced both youngsters and adults, holding their attention through the years until the movie palace became America's home-away-from-home.

Card games evolved from the traditional playing cards and, like jigsaw puzzles, served an educational purpose. By the end of the nineteenth century, the concept of card games had expanded to include dice, counters, board games, and novelty features.

Two Negro Dudes (company's title) from the A. Schoenhut Humpty Dumpty Circus. Other black figures made for this toy group include an African Chief and African Native. *Collection of and photo by Evelyn Ackerman.*

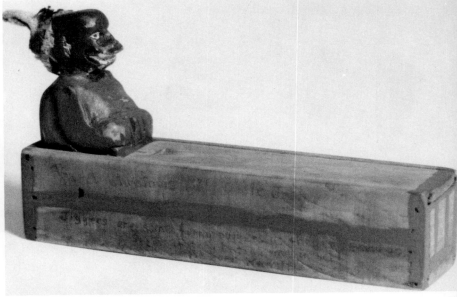

(Above)
Pencil box with black man seated inside. The box is painted bright blue, the man's torso is dull red, his cap is beige with red ribbon. Inside the box is written: "To Albert Christmas 1881 Uncle Josh. Jiggers are some funny puggers as they come and go. Seems is they'd stay home in bed no one would ever know." *Photo courtesy of collection of Barbara Kramer.*

(Top left)
"Jiggling Niggers," an unusual pair of dancing, jointed figures, mounted on a double board. *Courtesy of Bonner's Barn; photo by Robideau Studios.*

(Left)
"Jazzbo Jim," tin mechanical toy. *Courtesy of Bonner's Barn; photo by Robideau Studios.*

KINDS OF TOYS

AUTOMATA

Automatic devices go back as far as the ancient Romans, who had a device that opened temple doors. Clocks were popular in the thirteenth-century Mongol court and continued their popularity throughout the sixteenth and seventeenth centuries. The eighteenth and nineteenth centuries introduced figures that moved as a music box played.

An American firm, E. R. Ives of Bridgeport, Connecticut, made automated dolls that included one called Uncle Tom and another called Heathen Chinee. Black automata are fairly rare so that when a collector finds one, he/she has reason to be excited. Most of the good automata can be found in toy museums, such as the Shelburne Museum in Vermont.

Clockmakers were often noted as being able to make automated toys as well and some of these are not marked with the maker's name.

BOARD GAMES

Most board games involve a beginning and an end, the participants competing in a race for the finish. The games are often accessorized with dice counters and paper money.

Board games made to feature black playing pieces were extremely derogatory in nature. Often the central black character was being chased by an animal or another human being, and usually the object of the game was to catch the black person. Whichever way you played, the Negro lost.

Some of the companies that manufactured board games were Parker Brothers Co. in Salem, Massachusetts, W. & S. B. Ives, and McLoughlin Brothers, and Milton Bradley of Springfield, Massachusetts. The Bradley and Parker companies are still in the business of producing board games.

Twentieth-century board games are sometimes marked with their copyright date on the outside box cover. They will also have the maker's name marked there and that information will help you to research your board game's origins.

Cards made for the St. Louis Southwestern Railroad Company are marked "Cotton Belt Route." *Courtesy of Jan Thalberg; photo by Donald Vogt.*

Crown Card Company made this card game called "Game of In Dixieland." Each card showed a different photograph. *Courtesy of Jan Thalberg; photo by Donald Vogt.*

CARD GAMES

The use of playing cards can be traced back to the Middle Ages as well as to early China. Although we usually associate card playing with gambling, there were a number of other uses for card games. In fact, monks were originally assigned their duties by use of a specifically designed card game, and in the nineteenth century, cards were used to teach literature, botany, and geography. By the mid-nineteenth century, card games for enjoyment became much more prevalent.

By the end of the nineteenth century, the concept of card games had expanded to include dice, counters, board games, and novelty features.

One can find an indeterminate number of card games that featured black people as card decorations or that were designed to be played under specific directions. Often such card games were distributed on railroad lines to keep the customers occupied.

MECHANICAL TOYS

In the first third of the twentieth century major department stores such as Sears, Roebuck and Company and Montgomery Ward sold mechanical toys that portrayed black people in an unfavorable light. Toys such as Musical Negroes, Alabama Coon Jigger, Mammy's Black Boy, and Dude Negro were advertised in their catalogues as "amusing" and "fascinating." For the most part, these mechanical toys were made of tin and were fairly colorful. See "Tin and Cast Iron Toys," below, and Chapter 3, "Banks," for more information.

PULL TOYS

Through the years pull toys have been made in the black tradition. One of the earliest and most interesting is a lithographed paper-on-wood boat on wheels that was made by the W. S. Reed Company and patented in 1881. The boat was 17″ long and held a group of smiling black men who played various instruments and whose arms and bodies moved as the toy was pulled. The side of the boat is labeled "Reed's Latest Sensation—Pull for the Shore."

Another such toy was made by N. N. Hill Brass Company around 1900. Made of brass, the toy features a bronze alligator on wheels. Atop the alligator sits a black boy in a blue jacket, yellow pants, and red hat. When the toy is pushed or pulled, the bell (or gong) underneath the alligator is sounded.

PUZZLES

Jigsaw puzzles had relatively large pieces and simple shapes in Victorian days. The idea of early puzzles was to pass on knowledge in an interesting way. Because of that, puzzles often related to history and geography.

Later in the nineteenth century, works of art started becoming more common subjects for puzzle makers.

Puzzles depicting black subjects became common during the latter part of the nineteenth century and beginning of the twentieth. Subjects were characters from books (*Sambo*), cartoon characters, and real-life, stage, screen, and television personalities (*Amos 'n Andy*).

TABLE GAMES/TOYS

This category includes rolling and tossing games, which were extremely popular in the Victorian era.

Bean-toss games often incorporated black faces or figures as the target at which the bean bag or ball would be thrown.

It is rare that such games of Victorian vintage are found in mint condition. However, they were made well into the mid-twentieth century and you may be able to procure some of the later ones in good condition. These games did take a lot of abuse so the chances of obtaining a large collection of mint pieces are rare.

TIN AND CAST-IRON TOYS

Because tin was light in weight and easy to work with, toys made of that material first appeared in quantity in the early nineteenth century.

The United States, Connecticut in particular, took the lead in this new field. As early as the 1820s, tinsmiths in Connecticut were making tin whistles and bubble pipes. Factories sprang up to produce tin toys within a decade.

Francis, Field and Francis, a Pennsylvania firm, was documented as producing black tin toys in 1838; the firm continued a decade later under a different name, Philadelphia Tin Toy Manufactory.

Clockwork toys were made by George W. Brown and Company in Forestville, New York. The firm began in 1856 and changed its name to Steven and Brown in 1869, having taken on a partner formerly with the cast-iron toy-making company J. & E. Stevens (see Chapter 3). They made a number of black tin toys, but their specialty was wheeled horse-drawn vehicles.

An interesting pair of clockwork toys was made in the 1870s by the Ives Company. The toys were drums and on top of each drum was a wooden dancing figure. One was a black woman and the other a black man, each dressed in colorful clothes.

Another example of a fine clockwork toy was made by the Automatic Toy Works in 1875. The toy, 10″ in height, was a black suffragette woman standing on a box. The woman bends forward, straightens up, and bangs her fist on the podium in front of her. The Ives Company made a similar toy featuring a black stump speaker in 1882.

Automatic also produced a toy featuring an old black fiddler seated on a stool, playing his instrument. He is dressed in a morning suit which consists of checked pants and a velvet coat. His hand moves the bow back and forth across the violin's strings.

A livelier clockwork toy is The Canewalkers. Two dancers of "colored society people" dance around comically. When first shown in the 1890 Ives catalogue, the dancers were sold (wholesale) for $36 per dozen. It would be practically impossible to find *one* of these toys at that price today!

The Ives Company appears to have made more black clockwork, tin, and iron toys than any other manufacturer of its time, and many examples other than the ones already mentioned can be added to a black toy collection.

The period between 1840 and 1890 seems to have produced the finest of black American tin toys, but companies such as the Marx toy firm continued to produce imaginative toys in the early 1900s and led the way with windup tin toys.

The Gong Bell Company advertised a toy in their 1983 catalog that showed a black man kneeling on an iron cart. The man was ringing a Liberty Bell. Could the slave have been celebrating his freedom? This combination of tin and cast iron was expensive to produce, thus the toy is rare.

The period after World War II brought us toys made in Occupied Japan and Germany (1945–1952). These toys, stamped with the maker's mark as well as the words "Occupied Japan" or "U.S. Zone Germany," are easily identifiable. Be-

Uncle Tom's "Topsy" marionette has an extremely heavy head, possibly of lead. An early marionette, she was probably made during the late 1800s. *Courtesy of Rose Fontanella; photo by Donald Vogt.*

"Jazzbo Jim" tin mechanical toy in its original box. *Courtesy of Jim Bollman, The Music Emporium; photo by Donald Vogt.*

Hazelle's "Minstrel" marionette, in the original box, was made in Kansas City, Missouri. *Courtesy of Rose Fontanella; photo by Donald Vogt.*

fore 1900, there were a number of people involved in the making of toys and the item was not allowed to be marked with the maker's name because the middleman's job (of jobber) would have been eliminated.

Cast-iron toys were not made as prolifically as tin. They were enjoyed in the United States during the late nineteenth and early twentieth centuries. J. & E. Stevens was a prominent manufacturer of cast-iron toys, cap guns, banks, and small tools. Also in the field were the Ives firm, Hubley Manufacturing Co. of Lancaster, Pennsylvania, and the Kenton Hardware Company of Kenton, Ohio.

Gray iron was used because it was sturdy and could be painted. Once the basis was laid, companies turned out identical cast figures and used standard parts, making it easier to put the toys on the mass market.

One such toy was the popular horse-and-buggy. The Kenton Company made a phaeton in the late 1800s that was 18" long and featured a lady with a dog in the rear and a black coachman in formal black uniform in front.

Cap pistols were often made in animated figures including Punch and Judy, Chinese figures, Irish figures, and black figures.

Framed Fairyland puzzles. The set includes Little Black Sambo. *Courtesy of Basia Kirschner; photo by Donald Vogt.*

A Little Black Sambo wooden puzzle dating from the 1950s. *Photo by Donald Vogt.*

Amos 'n Andy Fresh Air Taxicab, by Marx & Co., a tin windup toy made in the 1930s. *Courtesy of Kristin Duval, Irreverent Relics; photo by Donald Vogt.*

AMERICAN MANUFACTURERS OF BLACK TOYS

Chein Industries, Inc. of Burlington, New Jersey, started making toys in 1903 and is still in business. Their specialty is tin banks and toys. They have been known to make reproductions of roly-polys. They stopped making toys in 1977.

Edward Ives worked in Plymouth, Connecticut, from 1825 to 1930. In 1872, the firm became known as Ives and Blakeslee. They specialized in window displays, clockwork toys, horse-drawn vehicles, and trains.

Marx Brothers of New York began making toys in 1921 and continues to be one of the best-known toy manufacturers today. They made tin and windup toys as well as many other kinds of playthings.

The A. Schoenhut Company was founded by a German immigrant named Albert Schoenhut. He opened his toy business in 1872 in Philadelphia and began making lathe-turned and hand-painted wooden toys. His factory-made toys were often made in sets and replaced the customary, handmade wooden toys.

The Stephens and Brown Manufacturing Company of Cromwell, Connecticut, was in business from 1869 to approximately 1880. During that time they made tin and iron toys and banks.

The Strauss Company of New York manufactured clockwork and tin windup toys from 1900 to 1920.

PRICE GUIDE—TOYS

ITEM DESCRIPTION   *APPROXIMATE PRICE*

Alabama Coon Jigger, made by Oh-My Windup, Lehmann, 1912 .... $295–$335
Amos 'n Andy, ashtray with match holder, bronzed ceramic .... $85–$110
Amos 'n Andy, Fresh Air Taxi, tin windup, Marx, 8¼", ca. 1930 .... $350–$500
Bean-bag toss, black face, eyes and mouth pop out .... $250–$300
Boy drummer, black cotton hair over tin, grass skirt, 5" .... $75–$95
Clockwork toy, dancing black men, 1890s, American Mechanical Toy Co. .... $850–$900
Clockwork toy, dancing Negro man, jointed wood dancer, metal rod, wood stem, rectangular base with key, late nineteenth century, 9⅝" .... $495–$525
Dancing black man on stick, polka-dot shirt, checked pants, 1920s .... $25–$35
Dancing Bojangles, boxed .... $60–$80
Dancin' Joe, articulated toy, black man mounted on metal base, 15" .... $1,000–$1,200
Dan Jigger, black dancer, microphone, battery operated, boxed .... $400–$450
Dart Board, Sambo .... $60–$70
Five black heads, jump up and down when handle is cranked, 1860s, 11½" .... $100–$200
Flipover toy, wood sides and legs, paper body ...... $22–$30
Game, Card Party, Amos 'n Andy, score pads, eight tallies, boxed .... $35–$50
Game, child's shooting target, Sambo .... $50–$80
Game, The Jolly Darkie Target, 1890s, lithographed .... $150–$190
Game, Little Black Sambo .... $24–$30
Game, Poor Jenny, contents and box .... $75–$95
Game, Snake Eyes, wide-eyed picture on box, cards and chips .... $22–$30
Game, toss, Black Chuck, stands up, ca. 1890 ..... $50–$75
Hand-painted black woman, arms raised, dances, 1910 .... $235–$250

Hubley, cart, two-wheel, black driver cast iron, 5½" × 2" .... $185–$200
Kobi, Negro face, moving eyes, celluloid, 1920s .... $110–$125
Lead band of musicians, set of six .... $75–$100
Lehmann, African mailman, ostrich pulls black man, yellow cart, tin .... $275–$300
Lehmann, black man drives cart pulled by zebra, windup .... $350–$400
Lindstrom, Mammy, sweeping .... $145–$175
Marx, Charleston Trio, black man dances, other plays fiddle, 1921, windup .... $395–$425
Marx, Spic and Span, The Hams What Am, tin, 10" .... $475–$500
Pinball machine, black minstrel, bells, lights, Gottlieb and Co. .... $1,200–$1,500
Playette Theater, Little Black Sambo, cardboard, 1942, 18" × 12" .... $28–$35
Playing cards, lady, basket of cotton, boxed .... $6–$8
Porter, lead, from train garden .... $15–$25
Puppet, string, marked "Clippo presents Lucifer," made by Fleischaker and Baum, New York, 1938 .... $195–$225
Puzzle, Amos 'n Andy, jigsaw, 1932, Pepsodent premium .... $55–$65
Puzzle, Amos 'n Andy, Lightnin' Brother Crawford and Kingfish at O.K. Hotel .... $75–$95
Puzzle, Little Black Sambo, wood .... $20–$30
Puzzles, Fairyland, set .... $35–$50
Schuco, drummer, black man, windup .... $125–$175
Semimechanical, black minstrels, one with accordion, tin .... $2,500–$2,900
Strauss, Jazzbo Jim, windup, 1921, tin .... $185–$235
Strauss, Red Cap, black man pushing wheelbarrow, windup .... $40–$75
Tin, walking man, three different faces, 1925, 9½" .... $300–$350
Tipp Fireworks Co., Smoking Sambo, fireworks in Sam's mouth light .... $38–$55
Windup, Ham and Sam, tin .... $425–$475
Windup, Victorian cart, black boy on back half, complete, original box .... $240–$280
Wood, Shuffling Sam, primitive .... $95–$115

130 The oil painting that originated the Johnny "boy with the torn hat" Griffin novelty pieces. The colors in the painting are warm and soft; the painting is unsigned. *Collection of Joseph W. and Nathan Wood; photo by Donald Vogt.*

14

Miscellaneous Items

There are some black collectibles that do not fit into one category comfortably, or that might have deserved their own chapters had there been enough information to fill more than a couple of pages or enough interest to dedicate a chapter to the subject. Whatever the reason, this chapter will attempt to list all these "miscellaneous" items under one organized heading.

Perhaps your specific area of interest is covered in this chapter, perhaps it is not. As I have mentioned before, the field of collecting black Americana is vast and can hardly be contained in one book. I have touched on the major areas but am sure that as time goes on, more and more areas will deserve their own chapters in another book, or even command a whole book. At the very least, the following information should whet your appetite for more.

CLOCKS

Figural clocks, such as the female figure of Topsy, were designed around 1870. The clock faces were normally situated in the figure's stomach and the figure's eyes were designed to roll back and forth with each tick of the clock.

Chauncey Jerome, a clock manufacturer who worked in various parts of Connecticut, was known to have made most of the figural clocks available.

In an 1895 catalogue, novelty clocks (resembling later alarm clocks) with scenes on the face of the clock became popular. The figures in these clocks had moving parts—female figures scrubbed clothes, males played the banjo.

COMMEMORATIVES

Items to celebrate certain dates or occasions are often made in the form of a plate, cup, plaque, or other such thing. A picture, title, and date usually appear on these items. Normally made by collector-plate firms, commemoratives of blacks are becoming more common and should rise in price with the passing of time.

Each piece is usually marked with a maker's name and serial number or edition number. For example, "Limited edition of 3,000/number 159" would mean that the plate was the 159th plate made in a run of 3,000.

The plates and other commemorative objects that companies have been making in the past five to ten years are more colorful and attractive than such items were in the middle of the century.

COWBOYS

After the Emancipation, the institution of sharecropping, and the fact that blacks were still not able to advance themselves economically, caused a black migration to the north and west. Black cowboys were not a rarity. They drove cattle, scouted, and mined for gold right next to their white counterparts. Blacks founded towns in Oklahoma, such as Boley, Langston, and Summit. Cowboys such as Nat Love, who was nicknamed "Deadwood Dick," and Bill Pickett, the "Dusty Demon," were among the most famous of black cowboys.

DEROGATORY ITEMS

There are many derogatory items that fall under the umbrella of black Americana. Most of them can be considered part of one of the chapters we have already covered. However, one occasionally comes across a piece of black Americana that is extremely derogatory but does not fit in with items we consider to be folk art, or photographica, or even ephemera. The piece was made for just one reason: to be derogatory or racist.

I wish I didn't have to devote part of a chapter to this classification, but there is no denying that these items do exist, that they were made for many years, and that the prejudice/racism depicted was the norm rather than the exception for a very long time.

For those of you collecting such items, they are relatively difficult to find and can be very expensive. Every chapter in this book shows some derogatory items if you look closely. You must remember that one of the reasons prices are so high on items of this nature is that they are no longer being made.

Black papier-mâché Billiken, made by the A. Schoenhut Company of Philadelphia. *Photo by Evelyn Ackerman.*

California Studio Pottery made this highly glazed figure of a man and his guitar. *Courtesy of Judy Posner; photo by Donald Vogt.*

Commemmorative plate, white ironstone with black lettering, "In Memoriam, Dr. Martin Luther King, Jr., 1929–1968." *Photo by Donald Vogt.*

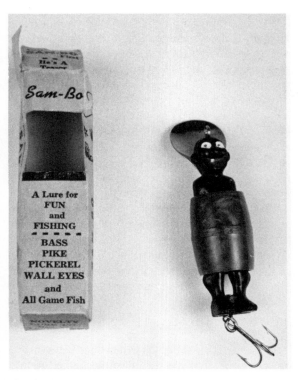

Sam-Bo Fishing Lure. Plastic, in its original box. *Courtesy of Kristin Duval, Irreverent Relics; photo by Donald Vogt.*

A brass ashtray/cigar holder, made in the 1800s, depicts Johnny "the boy with the torn hat" Griffin. *Courtesy of Jeanie Ohle; photo by Donald Vogt.*

"Bounty payment" due James Dixon for volunteering for the army (the 4th Regiment, Co. G. was a black regiment). *Courtesy of the Valerie Bertrand Collection; photo by Donald Vogt.*

JOHNNY GRIFFIN COLLECTIBLES

In the mid-1800s an unknown artist painted the face of a youngster in warm, soft colors. Since that time, a number of different articles have been made in the image of "the boy with the torn hat," or Johnny Griffin.

Brass ashtrays, spoon holders, pipe racks, souvenir spoons, chalkware busts, humidors, toothpick holders, as well as many other items have been made to resemble Johnny Griffin.

Should you decide to concentrate your collection in this area, you are guaranteed many pleasant surprises, because there is a plethora of "the boy with the torn hat" items to collect.

LAWN ITEMS

Water sprinklers in the form of black boys, lawn ornaments depicting black children, flower pots and planters, thermometers—all are lawn items made in the form of black people. One might also want to include hitching posts in this category, but they have already been discussed in the chapter on iron objects, Chapter 9.

Some of the items made during the 1930s–1950s—such as the lawn sprinkler—may still be found at flea markets and garage sales, but they are becoming increasingly scarce. Beware of the dealer who tries to sell you a wooden lawn sprinkler as a piece of "folk art." These articles were commercially made in large quantities and should not in any way be considered art objects.

MASONIC COLLECTIBLES

The American Masons, founded by Prince Hall, was originally an institution founded by free blacks. The Prince Hall lodges were first chartered in 1775 by England's Grand Lodge, an association of national lodges. Their rituals are identical to those of other lodges.

The Masons are a secret fraternal order, the largest worldwide secret society, whose members must believe in the existence of a Supreme Being and in the immortality of the soul. Their members wear a ring; the Masonic symbol is shown on it as well as on other pieces of jewelry.

MILITARIA

At the beginning of the Civil War, slaves fled to the north to join the Union army and fight for their freedom. The Union army, not knowing what to do with all their new black recruits, declared them "chattel of war" and in some cases even returned slaves to their masters. By late 1862, the Militia Act was passed and President Lincoln consented to enlist Negroes.

After the Emancipation Proclamation was passed in 1863, the War Department initiated the Bureau of Colored Troops. They were still paid less than white soldiers until the all-black Fifty-fourth Regiment served for a year without pay rather than accept the lower wage. By the end of the war, twenty-two black military personnel received the Congressional Medal of Honor, 156,000 black troops had fought with the Union army, and 39,000 were in the Union navy.

In 1898, during the Spanish-American War, the all-black Ninth and Tenth cavalries were the first to lead the charge of the Rough Riders up San Juan Hill.

During World War I, the 369th Infantry was an all-black unit that produced Sergeant Henry Johnson and Needham Roberts, both awarded the French *croix de guerre* for aborting a surprise German attack

The gas mask was invented by a black scientist from Cleveland, Ohio, named Garrett A. Morgan.

Although black soldiers achieved great heights during World War I, they came home to great racial tension and were sometimes even hanged in their uniforms.

Military collectibles span the gamut from Civil War discharge papers to photographs of some of the great black soldiers. Your imagination and knowledge of black militaria will show you which areas are easiest to collect. From there, you must rely on dealers and collectors associations in order to find the items you want to complete your collection.

REPRODUCTIONS

Among the reproductions of black collectibles being made presently are copies of iron banks, Luzianne Coffee items, souvenir objects, and advertising pieces, such as Coca-Cola trays. The best and only way to know the reproductions is to find someone who sells them, then visit that store or person and study their wares.

Compare the paint on the items you have seen at antiques shows and flea markets with the new ones. Remind yourself of the differences between old and new versions of the same thing. Is the new iron bank as heavy as the old? Are the screws that hold the bank together the same kind? Take notice that having the middle line a little off center is a characteristic of old screws. Check the paint. Are the colors the same? Has the paint started to wear and flake on the old metal? Old colors tend to be darker, duller. Train your eye to pick out defects. Roll the object over and over in your hand and study it. Educate yourself and you will never again have to ask, "Is this a repro?"

SEWING ITEMS

A little-known area of black memorabilia, sewing items have just recently been coming to the forefront as a viable collectible. Now, more than ever before, one will be approached at an antiques show by someone looking for sewing items, but I have yet to be approached by someone looking for sewing items that could also be considered black Americana.

Perhaps now is the time to start collecting these objects. If you do not have too much display space and would like to collect small black collectibles that are still reasonably priced, sewing items may be for you.

Neat little sewing caddies can be purchased to hold other black sewing items, such as pincushions or "Frozen Charlottes." There are a number of unusual and interesting articles that one can collect in this area. Have fun!

Mammy sewing caddy, made of wood, consists of pin cushion and thread and is marked "Lena, Illinois." It was probably sold as a souvenir. *Courtesy of Malinda Saunders; photo by Donald Vogt.*

A black "Frozen Charlotte" half-china doll sits waist-deep in a thimble-shaped block of beeswax. Thread was drawn across the wax for strength and smoothness. *Private collection; photo by Estelle Zalkin.*

A group of black pincushions. Sewing items are coming strongly into vogue and items like these will be snapped up quickly. *Courtesy of Jan Thalberg; photo by Donald Vogt.*

Black Mammy heads, or emeries, were used to sharpen sewing needles. *Courtesy of Jan Thalberg; photo by Donald Vogt.*

Souvenir tip tray from The Homestead in Hot Springs, Virginia. *Courtesy of Judy Posner; photo by Donald Vogt.*

A souvenir doll from New Orleans. *Courtesy of Malinda Saunders; photo by Donald Vogt.*

SOUVENIRS

For many years items from historic sites or large cities have been stamped with the name of the place and sold as mementos of the visit.

Many business establishments in the South, as well as towns, have had items made such as dinner bells, dolls, and "kitchen" souvenirs to be sold to vacationers or travelers.

One thing that seems to hold true for souvenir articles, no matter what they are or where they're from, is that they were cheaply made. Still the category is an interesting and varied one.

Silverplate toothpick holder, sold as a souvenir of the 1884 New Orleans Centennial Exposition. *Courtesy of Jeanie Ohle; photo by Donald Vogt.*

Mammy dinner bell was sold as a souvenir of the Olney Inn. She has a wooden painted face, a yellow scarf around her head, and a blue-and-white checked dress. *Courtesy of Malinda Saunders; photo by Donald Vogt.*

SPORTS MEMORABILIA

Since it covers a large area, there is room in this chapter for only a thimbleful of information on collecting black sports memorabilia. It is a subject that rightly deserves its own book. Perhaps its most important aspect is the black sports personalities themselves, for I am a firm believer that if you come to know the people, you will understand the subject more deeply. Following are brief biographies of some of the brightest black sports stars.

Muhammed Ali (boxing). Born Cassius Marcellus Clay in Louisville, Kentucky, on January 17, 1942, Ali went on to become a flamboyant and controversial boxing champion. He joined the Black Muslims in 1967 and later refused to perform military service on religious grounds, causing his conviction of violating the Selective Service Act. The Supreme Court overturned the ruling in 1971. Ali returned to a successful career in boxing, which did not end until he captured the heavyweight boxing championship three times, becoming the first in history to do so.

Arthur Robert Ashe (tennis). Ashe was born in Richmond, Virginia, on July 10, 1943. He was the first black man to win a major men's singles tennis championship. Ashe won a great number of tennis championships between 1963 and 1970. In 1970, he retired from amateur tennis and signed a professional contract. He has since been a spokesman for sports equipment and has become a wealthy businessman.

Jim Brown (football). Brown, born in St. Simons, Georgia, on February 17, 1936, as James Nathaniel Brown, became one of the National Football League's top all-time players, leading the league in rushing for eight of his nine seasons. A great all-around athlete, he played for the Cleveland Browns and has since gone on to star in motion pictures.

Althea Gibson (tennis and golf). Gibson, born in Silver, South Carolina, on August 25, 1927, became the first black player to win a tennis championship as well as being a moderately successful golfer after 1963. She won many tournaments, including Wimbledon, in her illustrious career. Gibson left competitive sports in 1959, married William Darben in 1965, and was elected to the National Lawn Tennis Hall of Fame in 1971.

Joe Louis (boxing). Joe Louis was born in Lexington, Alabama, on May 13, 1914. He was the world heavyweight boxing champion from 1937 until 1949, the longest reign in the history of the heavyweight division, and he defended his title a record twenty-five times. In 1954, Louis was elected to the Boxing Hall of Fame.

Willie Mays (baseball). Born in 1931, Willie (Howard) Mays was the second man in major league history to hit 600 career home runs. He played for the New York Giants in 1951–1952 as well as 1954–1957, for the San Francisco Giants from 1958 to 1972, and for the New York Mets from 1972 until his retirement in 1973.

Jesse Owens (track and field). Owens was born in Danville, Alabama, on September 12, 1913. He became one of the world's greatest track and field athletes, winning four gold

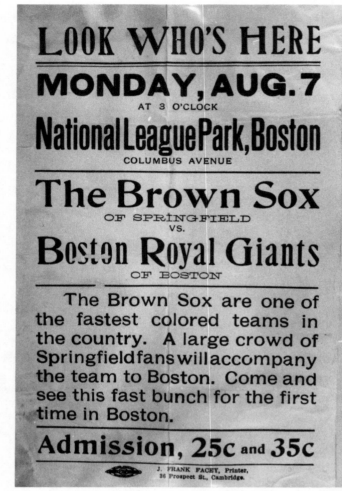

A flyer for a baseball game between two all-black teams, the Springfield Brown Sox and the Boston Royal Giants. *Courtesy of Valerie Bertrand Collection; photo by Donald Vogt.*

medals at the 1936 Olympic Games in Berlin and holding a broad jump record for twenty-five years. After Owens retired from competition, he held many jobs including acting as a goodwill ambassador for the United States.

Jackie Robinson (baseball). Robinson, the first black major league baseball player, was born on January 31, 1919, in Cairo, Georgia. He played for the Brooklyn Dodgers from 1947 to 1956 and in 1962 was elected to the Baseball Hall of Fame. An all-around athlete, Robinson also played professional football and baseball with the Kansas City Monarchs of the Negro National League. During his career, he was notorious for stealing bases, often unnerving the other team which had to try to prevent him from doing so. Robinson became a businessman when he retired from baseball in 1957. He died in Stamford, Connecticut, on October 24, 1972.

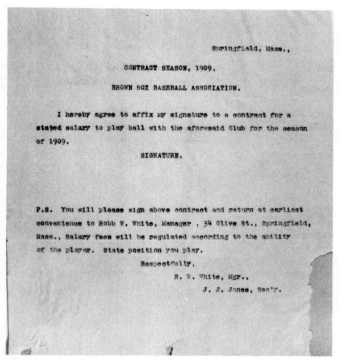

Original unsigned contract for the Brown Sox Baseball Association, 1909 season. *Courtesy of Valerie Bertrand Collection; photo by Donald Vogt.*

Autographed photograph of tennis star Arthur Ashe. *Courtesy of Mildred Franklin Collection.*

Autographed photograph of baseball great Jackie Robinson. *Courtesy of Mildred Franklin Collection.*

JACKIE ROBINSON, Dodgers

Sugar Ray Robinson (boxing). Robinson was a six-time world champion boxer during the years 1946–1960. Many boxing authorities consider him to be one of the best boxers of all times. He won eighty-nine amateur fights and forty consecutive professional fights before being defeated by Jake LaMotta. Robinson retired in 1965 at the age of forty-five.

Wilma Rudolph (track). Wilma (Glodean) Rudolph was born in 1940. She was the winner of three gold medals during the 1960 Olympic Games for track and field events.

William Felton Russell (basketball). Bill Russell is thought to be the greatest defensive center in the history of basketball. He was born in Monroe, Louisiana, in 1934. The 6'10" basketball star played with the Boston Celtics for thirteen seasons and later became that team's—and the NBA's—first black coach.

DESCRIPTION	APPROXIMATE PRICE
Ashtray, Amos 'n Andy	$75–$95
Ashtray, black boy on bedpan, china	$20–$30
Ashtray, black boy, "The early bird catches the worm"	$75–$90
Ashtray, boy eating watermelon	$10–$15
Ashtray, child on potty, metal	$35–$50
Ashtray/card holder, brass, Johnny Griffin	$225–$275
Basket, Mammy, iron, red dress, white basket	$55–$75
Bell, black figure, porcelain	$35–$55
Bell, figural, Aunt Jemima, bisque, 7″	$18–$24
Bell, figural, black girl, semiporcelain, 8″	$75–$90
Bell, Mammy, bisque, 5″	$6–$8
Bell hook, Johnson Hat Company, black man in top hat, celluloid	$7–$15
Bisque night light, head of black boy, paperweight eyes	$115–$130
Bisque tobacco jar, black lady's head cover, smoking pipe, 5¼″	$55–$60
Bisque tobacco jar, black man's head cover, smokes pipe*	$75–$90
Brass match holder and ashtray, black porter carrying bags	$45–$60
Brush, shaving, Mammy, figural handle, wooden	$12–$15
Butler, wood, holding rack of glasses, ca. 1900	$1,100–$1,300
Button, black man eating watermelon, porcelain	$225–$300
Calling card holder, boy, standing, in toga	$1,450–$1,700
Card holder, bellhop, full figure, floor-standing, 32″	$145–$180
Ceramic salve box, colorful transfer of "The Battle of the Nile" on lid, 4″ × 2½″, ca. 1870	$295–$325
Chalk bust, Victorian, young boy with Turkish cap, 15″ tall, ca. 1870	$275–$300
Chalk figure, young man shooting dice, made by Alexander Corp., Advertising Displays, Philadelphia, 7″ tall, 5″ × 6″ base, paper label, ca. 1940	$155–$180
Chalkware, black boy eating watermelon, 4″	$20–$35
Chalkware, black boy holding alligator's mouth open	$20–$30
Cigar store figure, black woman holding cigars, nineteenth century	$1,750–$2,500
Civil War memorial discharge, James H. Bryan, 4th Regiment, U.S. Colored Troops, Infantry Volunteers, dated May 1865	$385–$500
Clock, black banjo player, painted metal, 16″	$725–$800
Clock, cast-iron, blinking eye, Sambo, ca. 1860, all paint good	$1,320–$1,500

*I wasn't able to find out why the male version of this jar is worth more than the female. Chauvinism?

Dinner bell, souvenir, black Mammy, "from Olney Inn," wood, painted	$22–$28
Figurine, bisque, boy in outhouse	$7–$10
Figurine, boy eating watermelon, bisque, 3″	$3–$5
Figurine, boy on potty, boy and girl in nighties, bisque	$53–$70
Figurine, boy smoking cigar, holding hat, bisque, 9½″	$235–$350
Figurine, boy wearing jester suit, playing mandolin, 6″	$235–$260
Figurine, child on chamber pot, 2″	$10–$15
Figurine, child opens door, comical	$7–$10
Figurine, child, pink turban, arms out, 5″	$4–$8
Figurine, McCoy pottery, black man playing guitar	$30–$50
Figurine, stork carrying black baby	$110–$160
Figurine, three boys sitting on log, eating corn on the cob, bisque, 5″	$135–$160
Firecracker pack, boy sitting on river, fishing, eating melon	$10–$20
Hat, Aunt Jemima	$5–$8
Humidor, black boy, pipe in mouth	$85–$100
Humidor, figural, woman, gold earrings, headdress	$65–$80
Jewelry box, black boy shaking dice, wood, 6″ × 3″	$40–$50
Lamp, black man, 12½″	$65–$80
Lawn figure, wood, black girl	$85–$100
Lawn sprinkler, black boy, attaches to hose	$85–$105
Miniature iron black man, attached to cork with string around neck, handwritten note, "It's up to you"	$95–$150
Nodder, baseball player, Hank Aaron, original box	$18–$24
Nodder, black boy sitting between two oranges marked Florida, bank, 6″	$88–$115
Nodder, black child, blue dress, bank at side, chalkware	$350–$450
Nodder, black girl, sitting in rocker, nodding head	$145–$160
Nodder, black man, sitting in yoga position, coolie hat	$95–$135
Pincushion, black maid, lace apron, rooted hair, 7″	$15–$25
Pincushion, sewing, black Mammy	$22–$40
Planter, black boy eating watermelon, ceramic, 5″	$35–$50
Planter, McCoy, yellow flour scoop, black woman sitting on top	$18–$35
Plate, calendar, 1915, boy eating watermelon	$35–$55
Plate, In Memoriam of Dr. Martin Luther King, Jr., 1929–1968	$10–$15
Sewing caddy, Aunt Jemima, pincushion on lap	$32–$50

Sterling silver souvenir spoon, watermelon painted inside spoon, black boy's face (Johnny Griffin) on handle, "Atlanta" back of spoon, made by Charles W. Crankshaw .... $30–$50

Stickpin, black rolling eyes .... $95–$100

Tape measure, sewing, black man, celluloid ..... $100–$140

Thermometer, corklike material, figure of black boy, as is .... $20–$30

Tie rack, two black boys, ties in hands, "I rather guess we use some sense, We hang our neckties on dis fence!" Flemish Art Co., New York .... $55–$70

Toothpick holder, black boy and pineapple on one-wheeled cart, bisque .... $42–$55

Toothpick holder, two black boys eating watermelon, metal .... $25–$40

Watch, Jackie Robinson .... $200–$230

A handmade bonnet with a black face on back part of the head has features appliquéd on black cotton. The front part of the bonnet is polished cotton. *Courtesy of Rose Fontanella; photo by Donald Vogt.*

Thermometer shaped like a black boy with his pants pulled down. The material is cork—which does not withstand the test of time. These thermometers are easy to find, but not always in great condition. *Courtesy of Malinda Saunders; photo by Donald Vogt.*

This planter, popular during the 1930s, was made by McCoy in different color combinations. *Courtesy of Judy Posner; photo by Donald Vogt.*

141

Acknowledgments

My sincere thanks and appreciation go to the following contributors to *Collecting Black Americana*.

COLLECTORS

Evelyn Ackerman
California

Valerie Bertrand
Hamden, Connecticut

Rose Fontanella
New York City

Mildred Franklin
New York City

Diana M. Higgins
West Islip, New York

Richard Presha
Pennsylvania

Dakota Sands
New York City and Los Angeles

Jan Thalberg
Connecticut

DEALERS

James Abbe, Jr.
45 West Main St.
Oyster Bay, NY 11771
Specializing in: fine arts and appraisals

Jeffrey Alan Gallery
1568 Second Ave.
New York, NY 10028
Specializing in: American paintings

The Antique Dolls of Elizabeth Winsor McIntyre
P.O. Box 105
Colebrook, CT 06021
Specializing in: fine antique dolls

The Art and Frame Gallery
23 Main St.
Mt. Kisco, NY 10549
Specializing in: prints and artwork

Kenneth R. Arthur
David Copperfield Antiques
Box 219B, R.D. 1
New Haven, VT 05472
Specializing in: country antiques

Jim Bollman
The Music Emporium
2018 Massachusetts Ave.
Cambridge, MA 02140
Specializing in: musical items and memorabilia

Bonner's Barn
Robert J. and Florence A. Bonner
25 Washington St.
Malone, NY 12953
Specializing in: folk art and fine antiques

Connie Covent
Sign of the Windsor Chair
54 Buffalo
Clarkston, MI 48016
Specializing in: country items

Kristin Duval
Irreverent Relics
1048 Massachusetts Ave.
Arlington, MA 02140
Specializing in: country, kitchen, and black items

Anne and Martin Ellman
P.O. Box 26
Montgomery, NY 12549
Specializing in: Alaskan and Indian items

FairChildren New England Rag Dolls
Helen Pringle
Rte. 1, Box 82
Aledo, TX 76008
Specializing in: handmade, fine rag dolls

Gwendolyn Goldman
Gwen's Antiques
P.O. Box 151
Lafayette Hill, PA 19444
Specializing in: black ephemera

142

Gene and Linda L. Kangas
Box 175
Painesville, OH 44077
Specializing in: country and folk art

Bernie and Mae Kaufman
B & M Antiques
Malden, MA 02148
Specializing in: auctions

Basia Kirschner
P.O. Box 371
Newton, NJ 07860
Specializing in: black memorabilia

Barbara Kramer Antiques
1814 Bearss Avenue
Tampa, FL 33612
Specializing in: general inventory

Kenneth and Ida Manko
P.O. Box 20
Moody, ME 04054
Specializing in: folk art and weathervanes

Museum Antiques and Art
153 Regent St.
Saratoga Springs, NY 12866
Specializing in: antiques co-op

Jeanie Ohle
Slidell, LA
Specializing in: black memorabilia

Lucy Payson
Bell Hill Antiques
Rte. 101
Bedford, NH 03102
Specializing in: group shop

Judy Posner
Box 1124
Teaneck, NJ 07666
Specializing in: cookie jars and kitchen collectibles

Robert J. Riesberg
343 Salem Church Rd.
Sunfish Lake, MN 55118
Specializing in: fine antiques

Malinda Saunders
5406 9th St. NW
Washington, DC 20011
Specializing in: black memorabilia, promotion of black memorabilia shows

Sioux Antiques
Carl and Jeannette Pergam
8565 Cedar St.
Omaha, NB 68124
Specializing in: country antiques and folk art
    also at: River City Antiques, Louisiville, NB 68037

Joe Wood
Off Center Hill Road
Plymouth, MA 02360
Specializing in: art, folk art, marine antiques

Estelle Zalkin
7524 West Treasure Dr.
Miami Beach, FL 33141
Specializing in: sewing items

MUSEUMS AND EDUCATIONAL INSTITUTIONS

Howard University
Washington, D.C.

Moorland Spingarn Research Center
Howard University
Washington, D.C.

Museum of Fine Arts
Boston, Mass.

New York Public Library
Schomburg Center for Research in Black Culture
New York, N.Y.

North Carolina Museum of History
Raleigh, N.C.

Rhode Island Black Heritage Society
Providence, R.I.

Rhode Island Historical Society
Providence, R.I.

Shelburne Museum
Shelburne, Vt.

Smithsonian Institution
Washington, D.C.
(including National Gallery of American Art)

University of Mississippi
College of Liberal Arts
University, Miss.

Bibliography

American Heritage editors. *American Heritage: Three Centuries of American Antiques.* New York: Bonanza Books, 1967.

Ames, Alex. *Collecting Cast Iron.* Derbyshire, England: Moorland Publishing, 1980.

Antiques and the Arts Weekly. "Black Americana 1630–1984." Newtown, Conn.: The Bee Publishing Company, Feb. 22, 1985.

————. "CW's Folk Art Center wins grant to research works of Joshua Johnson." Newtown, Conn.: The Bee Publishing Company, May 10, 1985.

————. "Sharing Traditions: Five Black Artists in 19th Century America." Newtown, Conn.: The Bee Publishing Company, May 10, 1985.

Antique Trader, The. Price Guide to Antiques and Collector's Items. Babka Publishing Co., spring 1983.

Art and Antiques editors. *Americana: Folk and Decorative Art.* Billboard Publications, 1982.

Axe, John. *Collectible Black Dolls.* Riverdale, Md.: Hobby House Press, 1978.

————. *Effanbee: A Collector's Encyclopedia.* Riverdale, Md.: Hobby House Press, 1983.

Barenholtz, Bernard, and McClintock, Irene. *American Antique Toys 1830–1900.* New York: Harry N. Abrams, 1980.

Baskin, Wade, Ed. D., and Runes, Richard N., J. D. *Dictionary of Black Culture.* New York: Philosophical Library, 1973.

Black Americana Collector, The. Dec./Jan./Feb., 1983. Vol. 1, no. 2. Baltimore, Md.: Ronald Rooks.

————. Sept./Oct., 1984. Vol. II, no. 2. Miami, Fl.: Ronald Rooks.

————. July/Aug., 1983. Vol. I, no. 5. Miami, Fl.: Ronald Rooks.

————. Mar./Apr., 1983. Vol. I, no. 3. Miami, Fl.: Ronald Rooks.

Cederholm, Theresa Dickason, ed. *Afro-American Artists.* Boston: Trustees of the Boston Public Library, 1973.

Christopher, Catherine. *The Complete Book of Doll Making and Collecting.* New York: Dover Publications, 1971.

Collector Books editors. *The Standard Value Guide to Old Books.* 2nd ed. New York: Collector Books, 1979.

Collector's Showcase. Sept./Oct., 1982. Vol. 2, no. 1. San Diego, Calif.: 1982.

Curtis, Tony, comp. *Antiques and Their Values, Dolls and Toys.* Scotland: Lyle Publications, 1980.

Davis, John P. *The American Negro Reference Book.* Vol. I and II. Englewood Cliffs, N.J.: Prentice-Hall/Educational Heritage, 1966.

Dennis, Denise, and Willmarth, Susan. *Black History for Beginners.* New York: Writers and Readers Publishing, 1984.

Driskell, David. *Two Centuries of Black American Art.* New York: Alfred A. Knopf, 1956.

Ebony editors. *The Negro Handbook.* Chicago: Johnson Publishing Co., 1966.

Edwards, Paul K. *The Southern Urban Negro as a Consumer.* College Park, Md.: Prentice-Hall, 1932.

Encyclopaedia Britannica, 15th ed. Chicago: 1979.

Encyclopaedia Britannica, *The Negro in American History III. Slaves and Masters 1567–1854.* Chicago: Encyclopaedia Britannica/William Benton, 1969, 1972.

Ferris, William. *Afro-American Folk Art and Crafts.* Boston: G.K. Hall & Co., 1983.

Garrett, Romeo B. *Famous Facts About Negroes.* New York: Arno Press, 1972.

Gayle, Addison Jr., ed. *The Black Aesthetic.* New York: Doubleday and Co., 1971.

Ginzberg, Eli, ed. *The Negro Challenge to the Business Community.* New York: Columbia University Press, 1964.

Greene, Lorenzo Johnston. *The Negro in Colonial New England 1620–1776.* New York: Atheneum Publishers, 1968.

Hornung, Clarence P. *Treasury of American Design.* Vol. I. New York: Harry N. Abrams, 1950.

————. *Treasury of American Design.* Vol. II. New York: Harry N. Abrams, 1950.

Hudgeons, Thomas E. III, ed. *The Official 1983 Price Guide to Antiques by the House of Collectibles.* Orlando, Fl.: House of Collectibles, 1982.

Hughes, Langston. *A Pictorial History of Black Americans.* New York: Crown Publishers, 1956.

Jacobsen, Anita, ed. *Jacobsen's Painting and Bronze Price Guide.* Vol. VI. New York, 1983.

Kaduck, John M. *Advertising Trade Cards.* Des Moines, Iowa: Wallace-Homestead Book Co., 1976.

Kovel, Ralph and Terry. *Kovels' Antiques Price List.* 13th ed. New York: Crown Publishers, 1980–81.

———. *Kovels' Antiques Price List*. 14th ed. New York: Crown Publishers, 1981–82.

———. *Kovels' Antiques and Collectibles Price List*. 15th ed. New York: Crown Publishers, 1983–84.

———. *Kovels' Know Your Antiques*. New York: Crown Publishers, 1981.

———. *Kovels' Know Your Collectibles*. New York: Crown Publishers, 1981.

Lavitt, Wendy. *American Folk Dolls*. New York: Alfred A. Knopf, 1982.

Lipman, Jean. *American Folk Art: Wood, Metal and Stone*. New York: Dover Publications, 1972.

Livingston, Jane, and Beardsley, John. *Black Folk Art in America: 1930–1980*. Jackson, Miss.: Corcoran Gallery of Art/University Press of Mississippi/Center for the Study of Southern Culture, 1980.

Logan, Rayford W., and Winston, Michael R. *Dictionary of American Negro Biography*. New York: Logan and Winston, 1982.

Mackay, James. *An Encyclopaedia of Small Antiques*. New York: Harper and Row, 1975.

Maine Antique Digest. "Sotheby's/Phillips' New York American Paintings and Prints." Maine Antique Digest, April 1985.

McClinton, Katherine M. *The Complete Book of Small Antiques Collecting*. New York: Bramhall House, 1953.

Miller, Elizabeth W. *The Negro in America: A Bibliography*. Cambridge, Mass.: Harvard University Press, 1966.

Miller, Robert W. *Wallace-Homestead Price Guide to Dolls 1982–83*. Des Moines, Ia.: Wallace-Homestead, 1982.

Morrow, Lynn. *Black Collectibles*. Langeley Park, Md.: Karen Brigance, 1982.

———. *Black Collectibles*. 2nd ed. Langeley Park, Md.: Karen Brigance, 1983.

National Journal Antiques and Collectibles. Jan. 1983 and Dec. 1982. Allentown, Pa.: Constance DeAngelo, 1983 and 1982.

Official Sotheby Park Bernet Price Guide to Antiques and Decorative Arts. Ed. Charles C. Colt, Jr. New York: Simon and Schuster, 1980.

Patterson, Lindsay. *The Afro-American in Music and Art*. New York: Association for Study of Afro-American Life and History, 1978.

———. *Introduction to Black Literature in America—From 1746 to Present*. New York: Association for Study of Afro-American Life and History, 1978.

Ploski, Harry A., and Williams, James. *The Negro Almanac—A Reference Book on the Afro-American*. 4th ed. New York: John Wiley and Sons, 1983.

Porter, Dorothy B. *The Negro in the U.S.: A Selected Bibliography*. Washington, D.C.: Library of Congress, 1970.

Pratt, John Lowell. *Currier and Ives, Chronicles of America*. Promontory Press, 1968.

Robinson, Wilhelmina S. *Historical Afro-American Biographies*. New York: Association for Study of Afro-American Life and History, 1978.

Rodger, William, ed. *The Official 1982 Price Guide to Old Books and Autographs*. Orlando, Fl.: House of Collectibles, 1982.

Rodgers, Carole G. *Penny Banks, A History and a Handbook*. New York: Subsistence Press Book (Dutton Paperbacks), 1977.

Rosenblum, Naomi. *A World History of Photography*. Cross River Press, 1984.

Rutherford, Margaret, comp. and Curtis, Anthony, ed. *The Lyle Official Antiques Review 1982*. Toronto, Canada: Voor Haede Publications, 1981.

Sater's Antiques and Auction News. "Exhibited Black Artists Sharing Traditions in D.C." Vol. 16, no. 7. Pennsylvania: Sater's Publishing, Mar. 22, 1985.

Savage, George. *Dictionary of 19th Century Antiques and Later Objets D'art*. New York: G.P. Putnam's Sons, 1978.

Schwartz, Marvin D., and Wade, Betsy. *The New York Times Book of Antiques*. New York: Quadrangle Books, 1972.

Singleton, Esther. *Dolls*. New York: Payson & Clarke, 1927.

Sloan, Irving J. *The Blacks in America 1492–1977*. 4th ed. New York: Oceana Publications, 1977.

Smith, Patricia R. *Modern Collector's Dolls*. Paducah, Ky.: Collector Books, 1975.

Smythe, Mabel M. *The Black American Reference Book*. New York: Prentice-Hall, 1976.

Szabo, Andrew, comp. *Afro-American Bibliography*. San Diego, Calif.: San Diego State College, 1970.

Time-Life Books editors. *The Encyclopedia of Collectibles*. Alexandria, Va.: Time-Life Books, 1978.

Turner, Darwin T., comp. *Afro-American Writers*. New York: Appleton Century Crofts, 1970.

Wesley, Charles H., Ph.D. *Negro Labor in the U.S. 1850–1925, A Study in American Economic History*. New York: Vanguard Press, 1927.

Winchester, Alice, ed. *The Antiques Book*. New York: Bonanza Books, 1970.

Witkin, Lee D., and London, Barbara. *The Photograph Collector's Guide*. Boston: Little Brown, 1979.

Zeller, Leslie. *Book Collecting*. New York: Cornerstone Library, 1978.

Index